A GUIDE TO LOWERII
AND ELIMINATING DISTRACTION, AND BURNOUT

UNLEASH THE PEAK PERFORMER WITHIN YOU

STEVE ADAMS

Cover Design: Nada Orlić

Inside Layout: Ljiljana Pavkov

Printed in the United States

ISBN: 978-1-09834-141-1

UNLEASH THE PEAK PERFORMER WITHIN YOU

Contents

Foreword

My job is among the most stressful you can imagine. It is 100% results-driven, with 18-hour days and no vacations to speak of.

Winning equals success. Losing equals public discussions about my competence.

Don't get me wrong. There's nothing on earth I'd rather be doing than what I do now, as the Men's Basketball Coach at Penn State University.

Basketball is something I've lived and breathed every day for 40 years. While I'm always looking for ways to improve as a coach — and as a father, husband and friend — even I was surprised at what I learned from Steve Adams and my Tiger coach Scott Dillman.

I first met Steve in June of 2019. At that time, I was feeling anxious and on edge way too much. I wanted to slow things down mentally, be more present and control my reactions better.

In that initial meeting with Steve, I learned I needed to control my breathing in order to control my mind and my stress. Sounds simple, right? But I had already tried meditation and breathing apps on my phone. They didn't tell me if I was doing things properly or getting any better.

But I did get better with what Steve and Scott taught me, using many of the same ideas you'll find in this book. (You actually get access to *more* tools and insights in these pages than I did.)

Among other things, I've learned to improve my heart rate variability, also known as HRV. I found out that 9 of the 10 deadliest chronic diseases in America are all correlated to poor heart rate variability. Before meeting Steve, I had bad HRV. Today I have good HRV.

As a result, I've completely changed the trajectory of my future health, as long as I practice the principles in this book.

As a coach, the primary benefit to me has been that I'm processing what's going on around me better and not as quick to react emotionally. I'm more mindful than I've before with my players, both in practice and in games. I think the poise, the calm, being level-headed — that was critical to our team's success last season, when we tied for the highest AP ranking in school history and were on track for our first NCAA tournament bid since 2011.

Was our success entirely due to what you'll read in this book? No. Our players and staff put in countless hours of hard work to get as far as we did last season.

But can this book change your life for the better? Absolutely yes. If you're open minded, hard-working and willing to make a few simple changes.

You may find, as I did, that the benefits of what Steve teaches go way beyond your professional life and extend to your family life. Today, even with the many unpredictable changes that our world is experiencing, I'm more "present" and less reactive with my wife and 4 children. I'm a better husband and father. It's just that simple.

The ideas in this book are both cutting-edge and timeless. They've helped remove the "resistance" in my mind and body, so I'm free to be the best version of me possible — both on the court in a national spotlight and at home with those closest to me.

I urge you to read and act on what you're about to discover. The changes you see in your life will be nothing short of revolutionary.

PATRICK CHAMBERS
Head Coach, Men's Basketball
Penn State University
September 3, 2020

Introduction

There was once a king in India who was a big chess enthusiast and had a habit of challenging wise visitors to a game of chess. One day, a traveling sage was challenged by the king. The sage, having played chess his whole life with people from all over the world, gladly accepted the king's challenge.

To motivate his opponent, the king offered any reward the sage named. The sage modestly asked just for grains of rice in the following manner: If he won, the king was to put a single grain of rice on the first chess square and double it on each subsequent square.

The king accepted the sage's request.

And the king lost. Being a man of his word, the king ordered a bag of rice to be brought to the chess board and began placing rice grains according to the arrangement: one grain on the first square, two on the second, four on the third, eight on the fourth and so on.

Following the exponential growth of the rice payment, the king quickly realized that he was unable to fulfill his promise because on the 20th square, he would have had to put 1,000,000 grains of rice on it! On the 40th square, the king would have had to put 1,000,000,000 grains of rice. And, finally, on the 64th square, the king would have had to put more than 18,000,000,000,000,000,000 grains of rice, which is equal to about 210 billion tons and is allegedly sufficient to cover the whole territory of India with a meter-thick layer of rice.

It was at that point that the sage told the king that he didn't have to pay the debt immediately but can do so over time. And so, the sage became the wealthiest person in the world.

This story illustrates the power of exponentials. A real-life example of the power of exponentials at work is Moore's Law. Moore's Law refers to the number of transistors in an integrated circuit chip doubling every 18 months. This means that computers double in power yet cost the same every year and a half. Intel's Founder, Gordon Moore, observed this phenomenon in 1965 and thought that it might go on another 10 years. It's now 55 years later and the Law continues.

The continuation of Moore's Law has resulted in technology doubling in power and dropping in price for decades, and there is no slowdown in sight. This is why the computational power of the cell phone in your hands is greater than the Apollo space missions engineered by NASA in the 1960s and 1970s.

Moore's Law has led to a concept Ray Kurzweil, Google's Director of Engineering and co-founder of Singularity University, describes as "the Law of Accelerating Returns." In layman's terms, this means that we use new computers to design even faster computers, thus creating a positive feedback loop, which hastens the rate of acceleration.

Due to this "Law of Accelerated Returns," Kurzweil predicts that the typical laptop, used by millions of people, will have the same computing power as the human brain in 2023. In fact, Kurzweil predicts that humans will experience 20,000 years of technological change in the next 100 years due to converging, exponentially advancing technology.

Kurzweil predicts that by 2045 we will reach biological and technological singularity whereby many facets of life, education, travel, and identity change in unimaginable ways. In their book, *The Future Is Faster Than You Think*, Steven Kotler and Peter Diamandis explain the concept of convergence. They explain that we are living in an era where formerly independent waves of exponentially accelerating technology are beginning to converge with other independent waves of exponentially accelerating technology, leading to innovation on an unprecedented scale.

A single disruptive technology, like the digital camera, forever changed the business model of selling and processing film for photography by Kodak. Streaming services are fundamentally changing the way people view content on their TVs, and the smartphone disconnected us from the traditional phone attached by a chord to the wall at home.

While one disruptive technology impacts a product or industry, converging technologies have the potential to wipe out entire products, service offerings, and markets. What does this mean for individuals and their work? MIT economists Erik Brynjolfsson and Andrew McAfee, in their 2011 book *Race Against the Machine*, make the case that labor markets are being transformed by the expansion of digital technology. They state, "We are in the early throes of a Great Restructuring... Our technologies are racing ahead, but many of our skills and organizations are lagging behind."

As Moore's Law marches on, the gap between what humans can do and what intelligent machines can do will narrow—think laptops having the same power as the human brain. As this gap shrinks, businesses will undoubtedly choose to buy more machines rather than hire people for unremarkable, repetitive, or low-knowledge content work.

In work that only humans can do, because of technology facilitating remote work, companies will have the luxury and opportunity to find the most skilled people in the world, thus the connection between the location of business and the local labor pool will become less of a factor. People will need to compete increasingly globally for work.

The obvious question is: Are you ready? Is the average-knowledge worker prepared for the potential need to re-skill quickly and adapt to this rate of change? Based on research into work habits and psychological states, the state of preparedness for most people is not promising. In fact, it's downright scary just how unprepared most of us actually are. Consider these facts...

In a 2014 study on workplace stress by the American Institute of Stress, it revealed that 77% of Americans report physical symptoms from stress, 73% report psychological symptoms, and 33% report experiencing extreme stress. Imagine what those numbers are now with only six years of technological advancement?

Chronic stress leads to impaired cognitive function, chronic disease, and lowered productivity, which means that pervasive stress among individuals doesn't bode well in preparing them to face the tsunami of change that looms ahead. Chronic stress shortens the number of years you have to produce at an elite level, thus reducing the time you have to build and live out the visions for your business or career. Chronic stress and its consequences reduce the number of healthy years you have to enjoy your spouse or significant other, watch your children bloom into adults, and play with your grandchildren. Lastly, whatever your bucket list is, if you fail to control your stress and adapt to change, it will negatively impact your ability to enjoy the experiences you desire thanks to poor financial and physical health.

From a health perspective, a large proportion of the American workforce is not prepared for change. Chronic disease is a major source of interference in preventing sustained high performance at work. Fordham University professor W. Raghupathi and New York City College professor Viju Raghupathi state that, "A chronic condition is a physical or mental health condition that lasts more than one year and causes functional restrictions or requires ongoing monitoring or treatment."

Chronic diseases are among the most prevalent and costly health conditions in the U.S. Nearly half (approximately 45% or 133 million) of all Americans suffer from at least one chronic disease, and the number is growing.

Burnout is another growing problem in the workforce. In a survey conducted by Morar Consulting of 614 American HR professionals, 95% of HR leaders said that employee burnout is sabotaging workforce retention.

Meanwhile, cultural expectations about always being available and "on," as well as collapsed response times on any sort of communication, causes everyone to feel time-starved. Always being on and available forms habits that lead to an addiction to distraction, which prevents quality time at work and learning. Email, texts, and social media all draw you into their addicting apps, preventing you from applying focused attention to your work and creating this ever-present time crunch.

The result of chronic stress, poor health, workplace burnout, time-starvation, and distraction is that we produce superficial, average or low-value work output. This kind of work is characterized by repetitive work that you can do while distracted: Writing an email, reading a report, texting a colleague. Clearly, the average American in the workforce, based on these facts, isn't ready for the avalanche of change and is in danger of being left behind.

There is good news: You can change. There is a path to thriving through the Great Restructuring. Cal Newport, Georgetown University professor and author of the book *Deep Work*, says, "Our work culture's shift toward the shallow is exposing a massive economic and personal opportunity for the few who recognize the potential of resisting this trend and prioritizing depth."

In order to adapt to the accelerating rate of change that looms, you need to instead produce high-value, elite-level work output—work of the quality that another person or business is willing to pay for; work not easily replicated by a machine.

> Value-additive, quality output work clients and employers are willing to pay for requires deep concentration for extended periods of time. It also requires you to learn, overcome struggle, push your skills to the limit, and have breakthroughs that yield value. This kind of output, which is uniquely human, is very hard to replace with a machine.

Professor Newport suggests in his book that if you're going to thrive in an era of exponential change, you will need to develop a couple of core skills:

1. An ability to learn new, complex information and develop new skills quickly to adapt.
2. Perform at an elite level consistently generating new, high-quality output at speed.

Based on Americans' poor health, inability to manage stress, record levels of burnout, and distraction and time-starvation created by technology, the vast majority are clearly unprepared to adapt to exponential technological change and its consequences.

> The ability to adapt to exponential change, by developing the core skills of fast learning and elite performance require three things:
>
> 1. Optimizing your physiology
> 2. Optimizing your psychology
> 3. Maximizing the time that you are in a flow state of consciousness

This book is divided into three parts: Part 1 discusses the physiology of elite performance; Part 2 explains the psychology of elite performance; Part 3 delves into the science of flow; and explains how to live a high-flow lifestyle for elite performance. If you work through each part of the book and implement change along the way, you will change your health, how you think, and put yourself in a position to achieve flow and produce elite work.

Working hard, working intelligently, and squeezing the most out of each day through good habits and time management are good habits, but they will not result in the kind of exponential improvement revealed in the story of the sage and the king. This incremental approach will also not be enough to meet the challenges you face from the kinds of disruption brought on by exponential technological change. To meet this challenge, you need to learn how to regularly get into flow so you can produce high-value, deep work.

To get into flow—a state of consciousness where you feel and work your best—you must optimize your brain, your body, and how you think. Getting into flow requires a complete restructuring of your habits and day planning.

If you're chronically stressed, have no ability to sustain attention due to poor health, and your devices keep you constantly distracted, flow and high-value work aren't possible. Attempts to drive this kind of growth while operating with a mindset of intense activity leads to frustration and, unfortunately for many leaders, burnout. This is where my story begins.

When I graduated from university in the mid-1980s, I was part of the exciting, yuppy generation. We were all so excited by the possibilities after the tumultuous 1960s, the economic stagnation of the 1970s, and the deep recession and high interest rates of the early 1980s. Ronald Reagan was elected president, promising it was a new day in America. A few years into his presidency, the economy began to grow rapidly, optimism in America returned, and this is where my career began.

I started at a Super Regional bank in downtown Detroit in the management trainee program. My dad worked at General Motors in manufacturing for his entire career, as did many of his family members.

My mom's father was a career military man, which meant that I had no models of a white-collar banking career.

So I dove in, full of ambition and curiosity. I loved challenges and learning, which led to embarking on a ferocious reading habit that fed more curiosity and growth. I learned about how to change my psychology, to employ good habits, to manage my time, and to negotiate, sell, and out-work my competition. This led to a successful run for a decade at the bank. In the mid-1990s, I made a major change and left my secure corporate banking job for the unknown adventure of entrepreneurship.

Our family of four—my understanding wife, an almost 3-year old and 1-year old—with no economic safety net, moved to Wisconsin so I could begin a new franchised retail business. Over the next 21 years, it grew into a large company employing hundreds. In the early phase of growth, I partnered with a couple of outstanding people, who along with solid leadership in the field, led to a great run of growing a successful business that continues today. In 2017, I sold my interest in the company.

For 31 years, I bought into all of the success literature of casting a vision, building a plan to see it through, managing time aggressively, developing leaders to accelerate growth, and managing my psychology. However, I completely ignored my physiology. While I embraced the psychology of performance, I failed to appreciate the physiology of performance.

As the years went by, my stress levels grew, especially through some tough times during the financial crisis years. Unbeknownst to me, my neurobiology and stress response system were working against me, not for me. Year after year of stress stacked, leading to what I now recognize as a full-blown case of burnout. According to the Maslach Burnout Survey, the gold-standard in evaluating and diagnosing burnout, I was in bad shape.

Burnout led to poor decision-making, judgement errors, irritability, and a loss of positive emotions. I felt continuously pressed for time and I lost the ability to focus my attention for any length of time. All of this led to a decline in the quality of my work.

I was physically and emotionally exhausted, I was growing more negative and agitated, which took a toll on my marriage and relationship with my business partners. It also disconnected me from my faith. Ultimately, I left the business and took a year off to repair my most important relationships and recover. While I personally own the consequences of my choices, I needed to understand a fundamental question: How did I get here? The answer to that question, in part, was rooted in the brain, in my physiology.

A year prior to me leaving the business, I had begun a program to help me better manage stress, but it was late in the process of me being chronically stressed and burned out—I needed a full reset. During the year after I sold my business shares, I did a deep dive into the science of performance as well as my faith to try to understand why I ran off the road.

What I learned thankfully led to my full recovery and a new company, Tiger Performance Institute. Our team's vision at Tiger Performance Institute is to optimize performance. Our goal is to help individuals move from doing superficial work to elite-level performance, enabling them to increase the amount of time they have now through flow and expand the amount of time they have later through optimized health. We want to help our clients meet the exponential challenges of the 21st century.

We communicate our vision through a simple formula:

Performance = Skill—Interference

Your performance is limited by the level of skill you possess as well as any interference you bring with you to a performance. Everyone has some form of interference. Mine was my physiology; my nervous system was chronically stressed for far too long, which led to behaviors that compromised my sleep and health, leading to poor energy and the inability to focus, ultimately interfering with my success.

For you, interference may be chronic stress like mine, or it could be ADHD, depression, anxiety, PTSD, anger, emotional control, or something on that continuum without a clinical diagnosis.

A chronically stressed and time-starved entrepreneur will eventually hit a wall—this is their interference. At Tiger Performance Institute, our work reduces and/or eliminates your interference so your expertise and skill can take over and elevate your performance to an elite level. If you want to experience exponential performance—performance that will exceed what you envisioned was possible—keep reading.

There is a roadmap to performance that leads to results that far exceed the effort you put into performing your best. It comes from the fusion of optimizing your physiology, psychology, and learning how to enter flow. Flow is a state of consciousness where you feel and perform at your absolute best. Another commonly used term for this state of consciousness is "the zone."

Flow is validated in research that spans the past 50 years. Flow leads to a 500% increase in productivity, 490% improvement in problem-solving ability, 430% improvement in creativity and innovation, 230% increase in learning and memory, and 100% improvement in motivation and life meaning. Flow also expands grit, persistence, empathy, collaboration, and cooperation—all skills that lead to success.

The great thing about flow is that it's something you can learn how to do, how to do it better, and how to reliably get into it as you develop skills, practices, and organize your life around it. However, to get into flow, you can't wreck your physiology like I did and expect to experience true flow. The paradox was that I was working harder than ever and getting less and less accomplished.

The person who chooses to lean in and make fundamental changes to his/her physiology, psychology, and learn the disciplines necessary to get into flow is rare. Most will ignore the trends, hoping that somehow it will all work out.

Herein lies an opportunity. To become this rare person, you have to set the table to be able to learn difficult things quickly and produce at an elite level. This takes optimization of your brain, balancing your autonomic nervous system, and developing core optimization of health habits that will give you the cognitive function, energy, and resilience to do deep work for extended periods of time every day and sustain that deep work habit over weeks, months, years, and decades.

My story was far from the sage's and his mindset of growing his wealth by challenging the king to a game of chess with an exponential strategy in mind. Where I was, I couldn't even think exponentially because my mind and body were depleted.

Like the sage, if you want to adapt and thrive in the 2020s, which some are calling the decade that we will experience change in technology on a scale never seen before, you can't apply old linear models of growth. We need to think exponentially. Attempting to adapt and successfully grow in a fast-changing environment using only positive psychology and linear productivity tools will lead to frustration, limitations, and potential burnout. You will need to change your mindset to begin thinking exponentially.

This book gives you a roadmap to develop the physiological, psychological, and habit changes to empower you to enter a state of flow consistently. The payoff will be elite-level performance, exceptionally high-value work output, and you and your family will be positioned to thrive through the Great Restructuring. If you learn to master the concepts in this book, you will have a massive competitive advantage. If you can sustain the practice of flow and high-value work, week after week, month after month and year after year, you will look back and find that you did the impossible.

Learning to live a high-flow lifestyle is key to employing the sage's strategy to your own vision for life, but first, you need to recalibrate your physiology. Research confirms that imbalances or deficiencies in physiology prevent you from entering flow states. The psychology of performance also continues to be critically important. This book will explore the fundamentals of positive psychology and tools to drive performance, and your challenge is to learn to integrate strong physiology with it.

Equipped with high-level physiological and psychological health, you are then armed for learning flow, the flow cycle, the triggers and barriers of flow, and how to live a high-flow lifestyle.

Imagine applying the sage's strategy to your own life's purpose. What's possible if you're 500% more productive? What novel insights could you apply from a 430% increase in creativity and innovation? What business opportunities could you take advantage of with a 490% improvement in problem-solving ability? How much more joy could you experience from a 100% increase in life meaning?

Consider the implications of living a high-flow lifestyle and being able to get in the zone at will each day. What is the value of expanding time in the present to achieve more while also increasing your odds of expanding time later as you live more healthy years? What is the value of more time to see your kids grow into their adult years, to meet your future grandchildren, and experience more on your personal bucket list?

The promise of this book is this: If you truly read it, implement what you learn, and repeat good habits day in and day out, you will begin to produce high-value work. You will deliver work that will position you to seize the massive opportunities that await the few people who prepare themselves to thrive in the 21st century's Great Restructuring. If you implement what you read in this book, it will expand your time now and give you a greater chance of more time later.

Robin Sharma, author of the book *The 5:00am Club*, has a quote that I love. He says, "No idea works unless you do the work." I suspect you are a person who has been a top performer in the past and wants to reach that next level of performance. My exhortation to you is do the work!

Join me by reading this book to unleash the peak performer within you. As you go on this journey, you will expand time, learn faster, and grow into a new, higher level of performance and thrive in this era of chaotic change.

Part I:

Physiology of Performance

Introduction

The premise of this book is that you will face an extraordinarily high level of change in the next 10 years and in order to adapt with it, you will need to be able to engage your attention consistently to do great work and perform at an elite level.

The problem is that American's aren't healthy and this prevents people from performing at a level where their able to produce preeminent work. The Center for Disease Control (CDC) and the National Center for Chronic Disease Prevention and Health Promotion reports that 6 in 10 Americans suffer from a chronic disease and an incredible 4 in 10 Americans suffer from two or more chronic diseases. These numbers factor into the staggering $3.5 trillion annual cost of the U.S. healthcare system. The leading causes of death from chronic disease include heart disease, diabetes, stroke, cancer, Alzheimer's disease, and chronic kidney and lung disease.

As mentioned in the introduction, professors Wullianallur Raghupathi and Viju Raghupathi of Fordham University and New York City College define a chronic disease as follows, "A chronic condition is a physical or mental health condition that lasts more than one year and causes functional restrictions or requires ongoing monitoring or treatment." The salient point is chronic diseases function as restrictions, which translate into interference. This prevents focused, preeminent work output that would enable you to thrive in this era of unprecedented change. The primary behaviors leading to chronic disease include poor stress management, lack of physical activity, poor nutrition, tobacco use, and excessive alcohol intake.

This chapter explains how your body monitors its environment and the toll that stress takes on it. You will learn about the brain and the role that electrical output patterns play on influencing your behavior.

You will also learn how sleep is a major driver of optimizing your health. If you're like most people, you occasionally or frequently suffer from poor sleep and have a limited understanding of what enables you to get a good night's sleep. In this chapter, you will learn about the three cycles to manage in order to optimize your sleep.

Finally, the science of heart rate variability is introduced along with neurobiology. Through learning how your body monitors and responds to its environment along with mastering heart rate variability, you can begin to manage stress properly and understand some of the drivers of behavior that can either serve you or work against you.

Chapter 1:

Unlocking Your Body's Elite Performance

"The great thing, then, in all education, is to make our nervous system our ally instead of our enemy."

—WILLIAM JAMES,
America's first psychologist

The Autonomic Nervous System—Why Dogs Don't Get Ulcers but People Do

Have you ever wondered why your dog can just shake off the stress of someone knocking at your door and fall back asleep but the argument you had with your spouse keeps you up at night? It has to do with the fact that animals are instinctual and one with their environment. They respond to the stress, deal with it, then return to recovery or resting state.

As humans, we have the unique feature of consciousness. Not only can we assess a threat and deal with it, but we can also filter the stress and put a label on it, regardless of whether it's accurate or not. We can make the choice to hold on or move on; we can decide to worry about the future and create anticipatory stress. This ability to create a story in our mind is a subject that you really want to understand in order to know how to implement changes in your life. Failure to learn how to manage your stress leads to chronic disease, which works against your desire and ability to perform at an elite level.

The beginning of your journey to decode performance starts with understanding the role of the autonomic nervous system (ANS). This is critical because extensive research has validated the notion that an imbalanced ANS leads to chronic disease, impaired cognitive function, and suppressed immune response. In other words, an imbalanced ANS is interference that prevents the performance you desire.

The ANS is a network of cells that controls the body's internal state. It regulates and supports many different internal processes, often outside of a person's conscious awareness, to maintain internal balance, which is referred to as homeostasis. Hence, it's your external monitoring system, measuring and sensing what you are facing, in order to keep you in balance with your environment.

Let's start with some basic anatomy. Your nervous system consists of two main aspects:

- **The central nervous system**: This consists of the brain and spinal cord.
- **The peripheral nervous system**: This contains all of the neurons outside of the central nervous system.

The ANS is part of the peripheral nervous system and influences the activity of many different organs, including the stomach, heart, and lungs.

Within the ANS, there are two subsystems that work in opposition to help you maintain balance:

- **The sympathetic nervous system (SNS)**: The SNS generally prepares your body to react to something in its environment. For example, the SNS may increase heart rate to help you to prepare to escape from danger. It's responsible for the classic fight, flight, or fright response. Some have also used the analogy of the SNS as our gas pedal.
- **The parasympathetic nervous system (PNS)**: The PNS mostly regulates your body functions while at rest. It's responsible for how

you rest, digest, and restore. The PNS is analogous to the car's breaks within our body.

Your ANS is concerned with the concept of homeostasis or a state of balance necessary to support health. Allostasis is when you're imbalanced and your ANS is seeking to bring you back into balance by activating one of the two branches.

Here is a partial list of what homeostasis regulates:

- Body temperature
- Heart rate
- Respiration rate
- Metabolism
- Glucose levels
- Digestion
- Blood acidity levels
- Water and electrolytes

Stress

Earlier in the book statistics indicated that 77% of Americans experience regular physical symptoms from stress while 73% experience psychological symptoms. Let's begin with a definition of stress that's simple to understand.

> "Stress is a brain and body response aimed at promoting adaptation on the face of real or imagined threats to a person's homeostasis."
>
> —Dr. Bruce McEwen,
> professor of neuroendocrinology at Rockefeller University

Professor McEwen goes on to define stress as good, tolerable, or toxic.

Good stress is when you have a job interview, a speech, or a performance. Your body adapts to meet the challenge and when the challenge is over, you return to homeostasis.

Tolerable stress comes from loss of some sort. A relationship is lost, a death occurs, or you lose your job. The stress response is activated, stays activated, or is turned on and off over a period of time. Tolerable stress can lead to some emotional dysregulation, immune system suppression, and damage to the body. In this case, even though you experience a loss, you have the resources to be resilient and you can resolve the loss, minimizing the psychological and physiological consequences of the stress.

Toxic stress is also characterized by something bad happening, however, the difference is that you don't have the resources to be resilient and you feel like you have no control. This lack of adaptive resources leads to chronic physiological dysregulation, and when stress is ongoing or chronic, it leads to allostatic load or "overload." This makes it so your body struggles to create an adaptive response. Toxic stress leads to chronic disease, impaired cognitive function, immune system suppression, and impaired performance. Chronic, untreated imbalances in autonomic function can also lead to fatal outcomes.

When you face stress, your ANS prepares your body for action through the "fight or flight" response. If the body perceives a threat in the environment, the sympathetic branch of the ANS reacts by:

- Elevating your heart rate
- Expanding the airways to make breathing easier
- Releasing stored energy
- Increasing strength in the muscles
- Slowing digestion and other bodily processes that are less important

These changes prepare the body to respond appropriately to a threat in the environment. But herein lies a problem: Humans are unique in how we perceive stress because not only do we react to real stress, but we can also create it in our minds.

Humans can activate the sympathetic branch of their ANS from real or imagined work stress, financial concerns, or relationship problems. The fight-or-flight response is activated every time we ruminate about the past or worry about the future.

When the stress response is chronically activated from these per-ceived threats, it begins to do real damage to our bodies. Chronic dis-ease including heart disease, diabetes, and hypertension are all linked to ANS imbalances. To quote Dr. Bruce McEwen, "Allodynamic adap-tation has a price, and the cost of this adaptation is called allostatic load—the wear and tear on the body and brain."

How we filter stressful events and manage day-to-day stress has a sig-nificant impact on the "price" we pay for said stress. The stress response is meant to be an adaptive or healthy mechanism to protect you, but when you fail to manage stress properly over the long-term, this protective mechanism then turns into a maladaptive or destructive force in your life.

If your ANS is chronically imbalanced, it will hinder you from becoming an elite performer. Imbalances in your ANS will war against your ability to concentrate because it lowers your cognitive function, preventing you from absorbing new information and applying it in novel ways.

Given the evidence that failing to manage stress literally will kill you, learning the tools in this book to balance your ANS is a core skill of an elite performer. To decode your own performance, you must learn to balance on demand, which allows your ANS to reduce interference and enter the zone more frequently.

Great visions take time. Focused work that is valued by the market that will enable you to thrive through the Great Restructuring requires years of consistent learning, good use of time, and your ability to achieve flow and produce preeminent work.

When you can operate with clarity and focus around your central organizing idea and stack days', weeks', months', and years' worth of productive work, you can do the impossible. The key to seeing your vision through is not dying prematurely or being compromised in your ability to exert energy toward your goals.

Chronic disease, impaired cognitive function, and low energy are your enemies. Balance your ANS so it works for you rather than against you.

The next piece of the puzzle in learning how to manage stress and keep your ANS balanced is understanding heart rate variability.

Heart Rate Variability

"Have you ever wondered what the health impact of a stressful day was? Will you perform well during your long run tomorrow morning? Is there anything you can do today that would improve your ability to have a better day moving forward? Heart rate variability may be the best answer."

—DR. MARCELLO CAMPOS,
MD and author of the *Harvard Health Blog*

One of my good friends, Dr. Tim Royer, has a great analogy to start the conversation of heart rate variability (HRV). When I was under his care to overcome burnout, he explained the value of HRV in terms I could understand.

He said, "HRV is like a rubber band; when a person has poor or low HRV, it's like an old brittle, rubber band—any stress exerted on it causes it to snap easily. A person with high HRV is like a new, flexible rubber band. When you stress it, it stretches a long way before it snaps. When you train up your HRV, your heart is more flexible to withstand the changing conditions you face on a daily basis, leading to better resilience."

Medical professionals, performance coaches, and athletic training professionals are increasingly utilizing HRV as a biometric for overall health with their clients.

Homeostasis is a condition of inner balance while allostasis is when you are imbalanced and the body is working to regain that balance. Stress challenges inner balance and as Dr. McEwen explained, the concept of stress is cumulative and comes at a price.

When you become chronically imbalanced, the price you pay shows in the form of chronic disease, mental health disorders, suppressed immune function, and emotional dysregulation. This is called allostatic load. Fortunately, you aren't powerless in the battle to gain homeostasis or inner balance. You have a tool that we can utilize: Training your HRV.

HRV is the measure of the inter-beat variability between successive heart contractions. In layman's terms, it measures the change in time between successive heart beats. Why measure HRV? Your body is constantly adapting to changes in your environment and variability is good. Let me explain further.

Heart rate is different than HRV. Heart rate is simply the rate at which your heart beats. It's easy to think that a consistent heartbeat rhythm would be good, but it's not. In fact, a consistent heartbeat is more brittle, which means the ability of the heart to "flex" is lower, therefore, it won't perform as well as a "flexible" heart rate in the face of challenge or stress.

HRV is a research-validated and accurate measure of the ANS and therefore overall health. HRV is a good measure of autonomic balance between the parasympathetic (recovery) and sympathetic (fight) branches. HRV also measures the input of the vagus nerve on the heart, enabling it to measure parasympathetic activity. The vagus nerve runs from the brain to the abdomen on each side of the torso and is the body's major parasympathetic nerve.

The vagus nerve is a major component of the inflammatory reflex that controls immune responses and inflammation during disease and injury. Decreased vagal tone is associated with increased levels of disease and higher mortality rates, thus when you improve your HRV, you improve vagal tone, leading to improved odds of avoiding disease.

Age, gender, health, sleep, fitness levels, and mindset all influence HRV and a higher HRV correlates with increased fitness levels, health profile, and youthfulness. HRV declines with age as autonomic activities, especially parasympathetic regulation, also decline with age. HRV is higher in active vs. sedentary individuals and regular physical activity can be effective in diminishing the decline in HRV, cardiovascular health, and vagal tone associated with aging.

ANS imbalances negatively impact your HRV level. Medications attempting to upregulate autonomic function work only on the symptoms, while HRV training gets to the root causes.

Health Connections to HRV

A low HRV correlates to 9 of the 10 leading causes of death in the U.S., including:

- Heart disease
- Cancer

- Chronic lower respiratory disease
- Stroke
- Alzheimer's
- Diabetes
- Influenza and Pneumonia
- Nephritis
- Suicide

The only cause of death in the top 10 not correlated to low HRV are car-related deaths!

A low HRV is linked to risk factors associated with these leading causes of death such as hypertension, obesity, glucose intolerance, insulin sensitivity, and stress. As Dr. McEwen said, there is a cost to cumulative stress and that's chronic sickness and perhaps a premature death.

HRV, properly monitored and applied, can function as an accurate and objective monitor of progression or regression of disease and health. When monitored regularly, HRV can be used for the prediction or early identification of acute sickness or an impending medical issue. In the past, HRV training required an expensive, inconvenient, and clinic-based means to measure accurately and monitor. Today, smartphones with app-based solutions provide easy-to-use technology to monitor your HRV. Tiger Performance Institute also offers an accurate and convenient solution to monitor and improve your HRV.

Brain Function, Frequencies, and Dysregulation

Basic Brain Anatomy

Your brain is a very complex organ that contains millions of neural pathways. The organization of the brain consists of four structures: the cerebrum, cerebellum, brain stem, and the limbic system. The cerebrum is the largest of these four structures.

The cerebrum is where higher brain functions occur such as planning, reasoning, problem solving, perception, and emotions. The cerebrum is divided into two hemispheres, right and left, which are further divided into four lobes.

The frontal lobe is where executive functions occur, including problem solving, planning, and reasoning. The parietal lobe is associated with spatial sense, orientation, recognition, and perception of sensory stimulus. The temporal lobe is where your language comprehension, visual memory, and emotional associations are contained. The occipital lobe is associated with visual processing of information.

Brain Wave Basics

Did you know that you're an amazing power plant? That may sound like an odd statement, but you are an electrical being, producing electricity 24 hours a day, seven days a week. The real question is how?

As you eat food, drink water, breathe, and sleep, your body converts all these processes into energy, allowing you to literally function as your own power plant! You can observe this daily. You sleep, wake, drink, eat, and breathe and as the day wears on, despite eating and drinking, by the evening, your "batteries" are getting low and you need to recharge them through sleep again.

Optimal performance happens when your body creates and manages electrical energy with excellent efficiency and at the core of these processes is your brain. The brain operates as the air traffic controller for all the systems running through your ANS.

Your main focus should be to learn how to actively assist your body to more efficiently produce and manage electrical energy, so your power plant is running like a Swiss-made watch! Part of the solution is to understand brain waves and optimize them.

Since your brain is an electrical organ, it functions at varying speeds. Speed is measured in cycles per second, known at hertz (Hz) and the spectrum of hertz is 1-35 for the six primary classifications. The six primary classifications are based on the rate of speed or hertz. Each performs different functions and leads to different symptoms and behaviors.

1-4 Hz: Delta—Deep Sleep

Delta waves are associated with deep, non-REM sleep. If delta waves dominate your awake time, you will experience drowsiness. An excess of delta waves while awake can be associated with psychological and neurological disorders.

4-8 Hz: Theta—Rest

Rest for the brain comes with theta waves. Proper levels of theta waves are healthy because your brain needs rest. However, too many theta waves lead to problems focusing, while not enough leads to exhaustion and a lack of recovery. These can both lead to poor performance during your day.

8-12 Hz: Alpha—Imagination and Creativity

Alpha waves contribute to a calm and focused state. A large number of alpha waves can indicate a level of creativity unique to an individual, which can show up as humor, art, or innovation in a person's field of work.

12-16 Hz: Sensory Motor Rhythm (SMR)—Sustained Focus

SMR is associated with being in the "zone"—the popular term for when individuals or athletes perform at their best. Timelessness, effortlessness, selflessness, and richness of experience are the characteristics of being in the zone. SMR is a major regulating power in the brain between your rest and stress states.

16-20 Hz: Low Beta—Intense Focus

This spectrum of brain wave activity produces greater awareness and high levels of focus. Your critical thinking, learning abilities, and problem-solving capabilities occur here. If too many low beta waves are present, recovery and sleep become problematic.

20-35 Hz: High Beta—Anxiousness/Stress

Our "flight, fright, or fight" response is rooted here. While we often associate this response as negative, we do need to be able to respond with this level of brain wave activity in a crisis. Excessive high beta waves over time leads to anxiety, poor sleep, and obsessive behavior as well as long-term medical and neurological issues.

The most important thing to know is that you can actually train your brain to an elite level of efficiency and performance by optimizing the electrical activity in your brain to gain the benefits of each wave speed and avoid the negative consequences.

Dysregulation

Dysregulation of brain waves reflects an under-responsive, over-responsive, or imbalanced ANS. Most people are born with a healthy and balanced ANS and regulated brainwave functioning, however, genetic factors and over time, environmental conditions and poor breathing, all impact brain wave functioning.

Some factors enhance our brain and brain waves (i.e., mindfulness practices) while others cause dysregulation. For example, chronic disease, lack of sleep, chronic pain, and poorly managed chronic stress are all conditions that can negatively impact brain function. When our brain wave activity is dysregulated, then negative symptoms such as attentional issues, anxiety, depression, and emotional control problems present themselves.

For an entrepreneur, executive, or athlete, excessive stress can cause your system to be over-responsive. This over-responsiveness might result in a difficulty of turning off your thinking. The inability to quiet your thoughts can cause you to have a hard time sleeping, leaving you underprepared to function properly the next day.

Dysregulated brain waves are major contributors to interference that act as a barrier to elite levels of performance. However, the amazing thing about your brain is that you can change it. That's correct, you can change your brain. The term for this is neuroplasticity.

Neuroplasticity refers to the ability of your brain to form and reorganize synaptic connections as it learns and experiences new things. Let's get a bit more into the weeds so you understand this. Neurons are the basic working units of the nervous system, and within the brain, neurons transmit information across gaps called synaptic connections in response to new learning. Historically, the medical community believed that the brain was fixed and couldn't change. Research has proven this false, because the brain isn't hard-wired. As a result, your brain is flexible and dynamic, and if you complete certain training exercises/programs, you can improve your brain. We will explore how you can improve your brain in the next chapter.

Circadian Rhythm

The ability to optimize sleep first starts with your attitude toward the subject. Is your sleep time the first place you steal from to get additional hours to do whatever you feel is more important in the moment? Do you struggle with feelings of unease or guilt if you get a full eight hours to sleep? Do you think that you have slept enough in the past few weeks?

A major goal of this book is to change your mindset about sleep if your thoughts on the topic aren't healthy. Sleep is the most important task that you must do every day. It's a force multiplier, meaning that you get more benefits than the sacrifice made in terms of time. Failing to get adequate sleep is a negative force multiplier for your health, meaning that you suffer a more adverse impact due to poor sleep habits than you do from most other bad habits.

If you don't regularly get eight hours of sleep a night, you have a lot of company. Two-thirds of adults throughout all developed nations fail to obtain the recommended eight hours of sleep or time in bed.

The 2015 National Sleep Foundation study on recommended sleep suggested that adults between the ages 25-64 get seven to nine hours of sleep opportunity per night. Dr. Satchin Panda, PhD at Salk Institute and expert on circadian rhythms, recommends eight hours of nightly sleep opportunity to ensure you get six-and-a-half hours of actual sleep every night.

The consequences of sleep deprivation are severe. Routinely sleeping below the recommended level destroys your immune system, more than doubling your risk of cancer. Lack of sleep as a lifestyle sets you on a path of chronic disease, including this lineup of performance-destroying conditions: type 2 diabetes, coronary artery blockages, congestive heart failure, and stroke. Additionally, insufficient sleep is a key lifestyle factor in determining whether or not you will develop Alzheimer's disease. Finally, poor sleep contributes to psychiatric conditions such as depression, anxiety, and suicide ideation.

Building Blocks of Sleep

There is more to sleep than simply going to bed and waking up over an eight-hour time span. This is certainly a good start, but a major study published in *Frontiers in Aging Neuroscience* in June 2014 demonstrated that as people age, the quality of sleep declines. Therefore, to continue to sleep well as we age (sleep quality, not just quantity is a major determinant of how you age), you have to understand what the building blocks of sleep are and how to manage them. I will explain them here and in the next chapter I will give you the how-tos of sleep.

Sleep Architecture

The sleep you get each night is hopefully divided into four states and should deepen as you work through the cycles. Both quality and quantity are important in analyzing your sleep. Most experts on sleep recommend between seven and eight hours daily, however, you can't accrue a sleep debt and try to make up for it on the weekends; it's still lost recovery opportunity.

In summary, over the seven to eight hours of sleep, you recover physically in the first half and mentally in the second half thanks to multiple stages of sleep. Here are the stages and what happens during each:

Stage 1: Sleep Onset

The better your bedtime routine, the better this stage of sleep will work for you in the evening. This stage is when you first go to bed and transition into sleep. I will explain later how to create a nightly routine to maximize this stage for you.

State 2: Light Sleep

You are just entering sleep in this stage. You become disengaged from your surroundings while your heart rate and breathing become slower and more regular. Your brainwaves also begin in slow.

Stage 3: Deep Sleep

During this stage, breathing slows even more and blood pressure drops. Your body temperature drops, muscles relax, and the blood flow to your muscles increases. Hormones required for growth and recovery are released during deep sleep and toxins are removed from your body.

Stage 4: REM Sleep

In this stage you experience "rapid eye movement" or REM. The brain is very active during this period—this is when dreams occur, and your body paralyzes to prevent it from acting out the dreams as your emotions are processed. This is a vital stage for mental health and cognitive function.

One of the greatest and most important tasks you have each day is making sure you work with your circadian rhythm to develop a good nightly routine to ensure a good night's sleep. Commit to your recover just as much as you commit to your daily goals!

Recent Research

Dr. Satchin Panda is a leading expert in the field of circadian research and professor at the Salk Institute. Dr. Panda has established that there are circadian clocks in every cell of our bodies; it's not simply a brain function of tracking whether or not it's day or night.

We all understand what it's like to travel, change time zones, and feel off. I've been to 30 different countries, crossing multiple time zones hundreds of times in my adult life and each time I went on those trips, every cell in my body had to readjust to the day-cycle clock.

Dr. Panda's work has revealed that there are three cycles each day to be aware of and manage:

1. Our circadian clock for sleep
2. Our digestive clock for eating
3. Timing our exercise to work withing our sleep and eating clocks

It's not enough to simply time our sleep/wake times; we also need to integrate our sleep/wake cycle with our movement and eating cycles for optimal sleep and overall health. Failure to do this, especially our eating cycle, leads to poor sleep and chronic disease.

Dr. Panda established in his research that the timing of how we eat has profound consequences for our sleep, health, and how we age. In the next chapter we will explain how to use this information to optimize your sleep.

Neurobiology

The science of elite performance must include the discussion of neurobiology and the key brain signal messengers called neurotransmitters. The goal of this section of the book is not to make you an expert on neurotransmitters, nor is this an exhaustive discussion of the topic, instead, it's important to understand neurotransmitters' role in your performance, including flow states and lifestyle elements, which act to lower the risk of severe imbalances in your neurotransmitters.

A neurotransmitter is defined as a chemical messenger that carries, boosts, and balances signals between neurons, or nerve cells, and other cells in the body. These chemical messengers can affect a wide variety of both physical and psychological functions including heart rate, sleep, appetite, mood, and fear. Billions of neurotransmitter molecules work constantly to keep our brains functioning, managing everything from our breathing to our heartbeat to our learning and concentration levels.

Neurotransmitter Function

For neurons to send messages throughout the body they need to be able to communicate to transmit signals. However, neurons are not connected. At the end of each neuron is a tiny gap called a synapse and in order to communicate with the next cell, the signal needs to be able to cross this small space. This occurs through a process known as neurotransmission.

When an electrical signal reaches the end of a neuron, it triggers the release of small sacs that contain the neurotransmitters. These sacs release neurotransmitters into the synapse, where they then move across the gap toward the adjacent cells. These cells contain receptors where the neurotransmitters can bind and trigger changes in the receiving cells.

After release, the neurotransmitter crosses the synaptic gap and attaches to the receptor site on the other neuron, either exciting or inhibiting the receiving neuron, depending on what the neurotransmitter is. This is analogous to putting a password in and unlocking the account on a website. Excitatory neurotransmitters can bind to receptors and cause an electrical signal to be transmitted into the cell while inhibitory neurotransmitters block the signal from continuing, preventing the message from being carried out.

Neurotransmitters can be further classified by their function within the body.

Excitatory Neurotransmitters

These types of neurotransmitters have excitatory effects on the neuron, meaning they increase the likelihood that the neuron will spike or impulse. Some of the major excitatory neurotransmitters include epinephrine and norepinephrine.

Inhibitory Neurotransmitters

These types of neurotransmitters have inhibitory effects on the neuron, meaning they decrease the likelihood that the neuron will fire an impulse. Some of the major inhibitory neurotransmitters include serotonin and gamma-aminobutyric acid (GABA).

Some neurotransmitters, such as acetylcholine and dopamine, can create both excitatory and inhibitory effects depending upon the type of receptors that are present.

Major Types of Neurotransmitters

Neurotransmitters can be categorized into one of six types and from this list you can understand how they play a role in improving performance.

Amino Acids

- **Gamma-aminobutyric acid (GABA)** acts as the body's main inhibitory chemical messenger. It contributes to vision, motor control, and plays a role in the regulation of anxiety. GABA neurotransmitters increase feelings of relaxation and calm.
- **Glutamate** is the most plentiful neurotransmitter found in the nervous system where it plays a role in cognitive functions such as memory and learning.

Peptides

- **Oxytocin** is both a hormone and a neurotransmitter. It's produced by the hypothalamus and plays a role in social recognition, bonding, and sexual reproduction.
- **Endorphins** are neurotransmitters than inhibit the transmission of pain signals and promote feelings of euphoria. These chemical messengers are produced naturally by the body in response to pain, but they can also be triggered by other activities such as aerobic exercise. For example, experiencing a "runner's high" is one of the pleasurable feelings generated by the production of endorphins.

Monoamine

- **Epinephrine** is considered both a hormone and a neurotransmitter. Generally, epinephrine (adrenaline) is a stress hormone that is released by the adrenal system.
- **Norepinephrine** is a neurotransmitter that plays an important role in alertness and is involved in the body's fight or flight response. Its role is to help mobilize the body and brain to take action in times of danger or stress. Levels of this neurotransmitter are typically lowest during sleep and highest during times of stress.
- **Histamine** acts as a neurotransmitter in the brain and spinal cord. It plays a role in allergic reactions and is produced as part of the immune system's response to pathogens.

- **Dopamine** plays an important role in the coordination of body movements. Dopamine is also involved in reward, motivation, and addictions.
- **Serotonin** plays an important role in regulating and modulating mood, sleep, anxiety, sexuality, and appetite.

Purines

- **Adenosine** acts as a neuromodulator in the brain and is involved in suppressing arousal and improving sleep.
- **Adenosine triphosphate (ATP)** acts as a neurotransmitter in the central and peripheral nervous systems. It plays a role in autonomic control, sensory transduction, and communication with glial cells. Research suggests it may also have a part in some neurological problems including pain, trauma, and neurodegenerative disorders.

Gasotransmitters

- **Nitric oxide** plays a role in affecting smooth muscles by relaxing them to allow blood vessels to dilate and increase blood flow to certain areas of the body. Nitric oxide is also an integral part of the flow cycle.
- **Carbon monoxide** is usually known as being a colorless, odorless gas that can have toxic and potentially fatal effects when people are exposed to high levels of the substance. However, it's also produced naturally by the body where it acts as a neurotransmitter that helps modulate the body's inflammatory response.

Acetylcholine

- **Acetylcholine** is the only neurotransmitter in its class. It's found in both the central and peripheral nervous systems and is the primary neurotransmitter associated with motor neurons. It plays a role in muscle movements as well as memory and learning.

Now that you understand some basics about the chemical messengers in your body, let's transition to what we will discuss in-depth later in the book: The concept of flow and how it relates to neurobiology.

If you've ever pushed your athletic ability in a sport or played on a sports team, then you've more than likely experienced being in a flow state. A flow state is only accessed when you're completely focused and in the zone, often when risk or consequence is involved. It produces a feeling that conquers all other feelings and allows you to perform at your best, physically and mentally. The more challenging the task, the higher the likelihood of inducing a flow state, like skiing down a mountain.

"As skiers, we sure as hell know what it feels like after you ski an incredible line of deep powder or perhaps steep and technical terrain where your abilities are being pushed and your heart can't help but race with excitement. The lines where the inner chatter in your mind is silent and you are completely and utterly dialed in to the run in front of you, engaged and flowing down the mountain with a meditative charge."

—Martin Kuprianowicz,
ski enthusiast

Flow can be described as an "optimal state of consciousness where we feel our best and perform our best." It's been proven that flow contributes to overall human happiness and well-being in addition to being necessary to truly heighten your ability to perform any demanding activity.

Advances in modern neuroscience give us a greater understanding of a distinct pattern in the brain of how a flow state is catalyzed. Flow states start and progress via interactions between five different neurotransmitters within the human brain. The neurotransmitters are:

Dopamine—When you first enter into flow, dopamine floods your brain. It increases attention, information flow, and pattern recognition. It's essentially a skill booster, and flow follows focus, thus dopamine is a critical facilitator of flow and deep work.

Norepinephrine—This triggers the body in such a way that we have more energy, increasing arousal, attention, and emotional control, which produces a high.

Endorphins—From the word "endogenous," meaning internal to the body, endorphins relieve pain and induce pleasure. They function similarly to opioids, however, the feeling attainted from endorphins is up to 100 times more powerful than morphine.

Anandamide—Anandamide is an internal cannabinoid that feels similar to the psychoactive effect found in marijuana. Anandamide is released in exercise-induced flow states and elevates mood, relieves pain, dilates blood vessels, and aids in respiration. It has also been proven to amplify lateral thinking, or the ability to link disparate ideas together.

Serotonin—At the end of a flow state, serotonin fills the brain, producing a warm, satisfied effect. This leaves you with a post-exercise feeling of bliss and is only felt once the flow state has already come and gone.

Overall, these five chemicals make up the brain science of flow states. When you do whatever it is you do that gets you into a flow state, you can now recognize the science behind this powerful tool that's found within your own being.

Understanding the role and function of neurotransmitters leads one to internalize how all of the tools in this book relate to one another. For example, daily movement gives us more energy, and movement improves dopamine and serotonin in the brain, which improves mood, arousal, and motivation. All of these together improve attention and focus, and we know that flow follows focus. Your ability to get into flow enables you to learn new things rapidly and perform at an elite level.

As we move into the next chapter, the goal is to help you learn how to apply the science from physiology into easy-to-understand habits, which, when done consistently, lead to an increase in your ability to think and sustain deep, preeminent work. You will be able to learn new, difficult things and gain transformational performance improvements.

Implementation Checklist

- ✓ Begin noticing and eliminating excessive ruminations of past mistakes.
- ✓ Focus on today, in the moment, less on concerns and worries in the future.
- ✓ Change your attitude toward sleep, it's not something you can steal from, it's the most important task you do each day.

Chapter 2:

Eight Habits of Elite Performance

In essence, if we want to direct our lives, we must take control of our consistent actions. It's not what we do once in a while that shapes our lives, but what we do consistently.

—Tony Robbins

I remember it like it was yesterday: My wife and I were having dinner with our son Collin after his college baseball game and we could see the fear and frustration in him. He had had another poor performance on the mound, struggling with performance anxiety. To make matters worse, his academic performance was suffering as well. A couple of years earlier, Collin was diagnosed with ADD, which explained all of the battles with homework, forgetting when papers were due, or what tests he had to prepare for. It also explained the struggles I had as his high school basketball coach with his attention and focus during timeouts.

That evening, after assuring our son that we would find a way to help him, I reached out to someone who I recalled had used a brain coach and asked him if he thought that what he had done with his brain coach would help Collin, too. He immediately sent me the coach's contact and I was able to connect with him. This coach was a PhD who had a long practice where he worked with athletes.

The doctor began by training Collin in HRV. This is a core skill to manage stress and would help Collin learn to remain calm prior to performing as well as how to build resilience in the face of pressure.

Next, Collin began neurofeedback sessions. The goal was to get in three sessions per week for 30 minutes, but Collin was desperate for change so he trained daily, sometimes for as long as an hour.

About six weeks later, I was heading home from work in Virginia, where we lived at the time, when Collin called me. Our typical conversation lasted less than five minutes and usually resulted in him getting aggravated or impatient in some way, leading us to end the call. On this occasion, however, we talked on my drive home and then I proceeded to sit in the driveway for over an hour, continuing a wonderful conversation with my son. At the end of our chat, I asked Collin, "Do you realize what just happened?" He replied, "Wow, we've been on the phone for over an hour!" Not only was it a long talk, it was also a great talk.

Collin improved his GPA from a 2.2 to 3.25 that semester. That summer, he transferred from junior college to a four-year private university in Los Angeles with rigorous academic standards. There he played baseball for two more years, maintaining a 3.5 or higher GPA, while dedicating 35-40 hours week to both his team and a full academic load.

The transformation of Collin's life led me to complete the same training and experience personal improvement and our story is what led me to create Tiger Performance Institute. More satisfying yet, Collin is one of Tiger Performance Institute's performance concierges, who works with clients experiencing many of the same challenges he did four years ago.

Let's now learn more about this exciting yet not very well-known technology that changed the course of my son's future.

Habit 1: Neurofeedback

The first step in both my recovery and the improvements Collin made was learning to improve our HRV. Within a few weeks, we both began to utilize neurofeedback, a form of biofeedback for the brain that can be a powerful and effective means to create significant change in your brain, leading to improved performance.

How Can You Change Your Brain?

Neurofeedback is a highly researched and effective method to train the brain that originated in the labs at UCLA in the late 1960s.

Neurofeedback is the process of training your brain to use electricity more efficiently. It relies on your brain possessing the characteristic of plasticity, or the ability to change. The scientific method behind it is called operant conditioning, which is simply teaching your brain through a series of rewards and punishments built into the neurofeedback software.

As you train, your brain will change how it manages stress. As the brain frequencies are optimized, you'll experience better recovery and greater calm under pressure as well as have access to more of your creativity and problem-solving skills. Optimizing your electrical efficiency within your brain leads to improving the adaptive capabilities of your ANS as well, which has long-term health benefits.

The Defense Advanced Research Projects Agency (U.S. Department of Defense) conducted a study using neurofeedback to help get soldiers into flow states to accelerate learning and skill acquisition. The results were impressive: Soldiers experienced a 490% faster rate of learning and skill acquisition.

One of the core messages of this book is that there are physiological and psychological foundations that promote getting into flow states, where the next-level performance gains will come from. Therefore, anything you can do to build those foundations will enhance your flow and performance. Neurofeedback is one of the key tools to enable you to build a strong physiological and mental foundation.

Habit 2: Heart Rate Variability (HRV)

Breathe Life into Your Body!

We've already covered HRV in depth, but a brief review is in order before we get into how to apply this science to enhance our performance. HRV is a measure of the time gaps between heart beats as you breathe in and out. Variability is your friend, rigidity your foe.

Your HRV score is an indicator of how stress affects your body. It's also a measure of total load: sleep, nutrition, training levels, and mental and emotional stress. Finally, it's a measure of resiliency, and this is where heartbeat flexibility comes in.

If you have poor (meaning low) HRV, your heartrate pattern is rigid. It's like an old, inflexible rubber band; as stressors hit you, your heart is unable to flex with the stress, causing your "rubber band" to snap. Poor HRV is correlated with mental health disorders and poor emotional control.

On the other hand, good HRV—meaning on par or above with your age population—is characterized by a flexible heart rate. It's akin to a long, new and stretchy rubber band, which means your heart can flex with stress, strengthening your resilience.

Many in the performance world are calling HRV the best overall biometric that a person can utilize daily to monitor his/her health habits, stress response, and for understanding what needs to change.

What are the benefits of improving HRV?

- Improved resiliency and emotional control
- Improved immune function
- Stress is managed adaptively vs. poorly
- Learning is enhanced through nervous system balance
- Improved physical and mental performance
- Improved recovery
- Ability to fall asleep faster
- Decreased feelings of anxiety/depression
- Reduced blood pressure

What Is Measured?

Our goal should be to measure our HRV scores daily through a training program and apply those scores to modulate our activities and output every day. We want to gain awareness of daily HRV and then train it up over time.

How Do You Improve Your HRV?

Improving HRV varies (no pun intended) by the individual and his/her current health and fitness status. Active individuals will have more variability than those who are sedentary, thus, it's important to make sure you have an accurate device to measure HRV and work with someone who is trained in reading it to give you the best chance for success.

The most common starting point is learning deep diaphragmic breathing. This involves learning to engage your diaphragm, or belly area, to breathe in and out at a slower pace for a defined period of time. You can learn how to do this by searching YouTube for videos on diaphragmic breathing. The basics are first, place your hand on your belly and as you breathe in, push your belly outward. This clears the way for your lungs to completely fill. Pull your belly back in as you exhale, as this helps push the air out of your lungs. A good routine would be to complete five minutes of diaphragmic breathing in the morning when you first wake up, five minutes in the afternoon, and 10 minutes right before going to sleep. Tiger Performance Institute integrates this breathing into our neurofeedback sessions, providing our clients with a 20- to 30-minute practice.

In a literature review, HRV research pioneers Paul Lehrer and Richard Gevirtz explain diaphragmic breathing as part of a feedback loop that improves vagal nerve tone by stimulating the relaxation response of the parasympathetic nervous system. Lehrer and Gevirtz reported that people with higher HRV (which represents healthy vagal tone) showed lower biomarkers for stress, increased psychological and physical resilience, as well as better cognitive function.

Low HRV is correlated with nine of the 10 leading causes of death in the U.S. Additionally, a 2015 UC San Diego study reported that HRV may be a contributing factor for PTSD. The great news is that you can improve your HRV to help you combat any mental or emotional distress. Let me tell you the story of one of our clients named James (whose name has been changed for privacy reasons).

James served our country in the military and saw combat action that led to suffering from the effects of Post-Traumatic Stress Disorder (PTSD). James's struggles were common to most veterans struggling with PTSD: hypervigilance, anger, and difficulty remaining calm. James was a model client, putting in the work each day by completing his daily breathing and scheduled neurofeedback sessions.

You can improve your HRV and overall health like James did through additional means to compliment a consistent breathwork practice. We all hear how important sleep is and how you should follow the National Sleep Guidelines and get eight hours of sleep opportunity per night. Good hydration habits will also promote HRV improvements. Learning to reframe how you perceive stress or negative events can be impactful, too. One way to reframe is to start a gratitude practice and list things that you're grateful for each day in a journal. Another reframing technique that can be helpful to practice is noticing when you're ruminating on negative thoughts. When this happens, you should pause and name the thought, and then express internally that it's not helpful in attaining your goals. Slowly, you learn to move past those negative thoughts. Lastly, I've found that whenever I daydream or am just in a state of non-thinking (the default mode network in your brain does this), it's then that I tend to battle negative- or fear-based thinking. I've learned to be aware of this and redirect my mind and body, whether it be by walking, exercising, or engaging in a mindfulness technique like breathing to get out of the negative thought pattern. Negative, fearful thoughts pushes you out of homeostasis, and being chronically stressed depresses your HRV.

Learning to improve your HRV is a core skill you can develop to take better control of your health. If you wear health monitoring technology, such as an Oura Ring, Fitbit, or Apple Watch, you receive information each morning that can enable you to manage your overall load from stress, physical activity and effort at work each day. When you do take that control, your performance with grow significantly.

Failure to manage stress has a negative consequence: An overactive stress response and poor HRV puts you at a higher risk for type 2 diabetes, hypertension, cardiovascular disease, and cancer.

By mastering HRV and the practices that improve it, you're changing for the better for your overall performance and your long-term health for the future!

Make diaphragmic breathing a core habit that you practice every day and literally breathe more life into your body!

Habit 3: Meditation

Meditation and brain research have been steadily progressing for years, with new studies frequently released to illustrate new benefits of meditation, or rather, some ancient benefit that is just now being confirmed with fMRI or EEG technology. The practice appears to have an amazing variety of neurological benefits, from changes in grey matter volume to reduced activity in the "me" centers of the brain to enhanced connectivity between brain regions. Below are some of the most exciting studies to come out in the last few years that show how meditation really does produce measurable changes in our most important organ.

Skeptics may ask what good are a few brain changes if the psychological effects aren't simultaneously being illustrated? That's a fair concern, however, there's good evidence on how meditation helps relieve your subjective levels of anxiety and depression in addition to improving attention, concentration, and overall psychological well-being.

Making you an expert on meditation or telling you exactly how to meditate is not the goal of this section. It's simply important to know that there is real research behind meditation/mindfulness and that you may need to try different forms of meditation using YouTube videos and various apps until you find what works best for you. The following are studies on meditation/mindfulness and how it has an evidence-based positive impact on your psychological well-being.

Meditation Helps Preserve the Aging Brain

In 2015, a study from UCLA found that long-term meditators had better-preserved brains than non-meditators as they aged. Participants who'd been meditating for an average of 20 years had more grey matter volume throughout their brains, and although older meditators still had some volume loss compared to younger meditators, it wasn't as pronounced as the non-meditators.

"We expected rather small and distinct effects located in some of the regions that had previously been associated with meditating," said study author Florian Kurth. "Instead, what we actually observed was a widespread effect of meditation that encompassed regions throughout the entire brain."

Meditation Reduces Activity in the Brain's "Me Center"

One of the most interesting studies in the last few years, which was conducted by Yale University, found that mindfulness meditation decreases activity in the default mode network (DMN), the brain network responsible for mind-wandering and self-referential thoughts, aka monkey mind.

The DMN is "on" or active when you're not thinking about anything in particular or when your mind is wandering from thought to thought. Since mind-wandering is typically associated with being less happy, ruminating, and worrying about the past and future, it's a goal for many people to control said mind-wandering. Several studies have shown that meditation, through its quieting effect on the DMN, appears to do just this. Even when the mind does start to wander, because of the new connections that form, meditators are better at snapping back out of it and focusing on the present.

Meditation's Effects Rival Antidepressants for Depression, Anxiety

A review study in 2014 at Johns Hopkins looked at the relationship between mindfulness meditation and its ability to reduce symptoms of depression, anxiety, and pain. Researcher Madhav Goyal and his team found that the effect size of meditation was moderate. If moderate sounds low, keep in mind that the effect size for antidepressants is also moderate, which makes the effect of meditation sound impressive. Meditation is, after all, an active form of brain training.

"A lot of people have this idea that meditation means sitting down and doing nothing," says Goyal. "But that's not true. Meditation is an active training of the mind to increase awareness, and different meditation programs approach this in different ways."

Meditation isn't a magic bullet for depression, as no treatment is, but it's one of the tools that may help manage symptoms.

Meditation May Lead to Volume Changes in Key Areas of the Brain

In 2011, Sara Lazar and her team at Harvard found that mindfulness meditation can actually change the structure of the brain. Eight weeks of Mindfulness-Based Stress Reduction (MBSR) was found to increase cortical thickness in the hippocampus, which governs learning and memory, and in certain areas of the brain that play roles in emotion regulation and self-referential processing. There were also decreases in brain cell volume in the amygdala, which is responsible for fear, anxiety, and stress, and these changes matched the participants' self-reports of their stress levels, indicating that meditation not only changes the brain, but it also changes our subjective perception and feelings as well. In fact, a follow-up study by Lazar's team found that after meditation training, changes in brain areas linked to mood and arousal were also linked to improvements in how participants said they felt, i.e., their psychological well-being. So, for anyone who says that activated blobs in the brain don't necessarily mean anything, your subjective experience (improved mood and well-being) does indeed seem shift through meditation as well.

Just a Few Days of Meditation Training Improves Concentration and Attention

Having problems concentrating isn't just a kid thing, it affects millions of adults as well, whether they have an ADD diagnosis or not. Interestingly, but not surprisingly, one of the central benefits of meditation is that it improves attention and concentration. A 2011 study by Alberto Chiesa revealed that mediation is associated with significant improvements in sustained attention, selective and executive attention, as well as working memory. Since the strong focus of attention (on an object, idea, or activity) is one of the central aims of meditation, it's not surprising that meditation helps people's cognitive skills on the job, too.

Meditation Reduces Anxiety—and Social Anxiety

A lot of people start meditating for its benefits in stress reduction and there's quite a bit of evidence to support this rationale. There's a newer sub-genre of meditation, mentioned earlier, called Mindfulness-Based Stress Reduction (MBSR), developed by Jon Kabat-Zinn at the University of Massachusetts' Center for Mindfulness (now available all over the country), that aims to reduce a person's stress level, physically and mentally. Studies have shown its benefits in reducing anxiety, even years after the initial eight-week course was complete. Research has also shown that mindfulness meditation, in contrast to attending to the breath only, can reduce anxiety and that these changes seem to be mediated through the brain regions associated with those self-referential ("me-centered") thoughts. Mindfulness meditation has also been shown to help people with social anxiety disorder; a Stanford University team found that MBSR brought about changes in brain regions involved in attention as well as relief from symptoms of social anxiety.

Meditation Positively Impacts Cellular Aging

Elizabeth Blackburn, the Nobel Prize in Physiology winner, along with Elissa Epel, studied the impact of meditation/mindfulness on telomere length. Telomeres are the protective caps to DNA strands and are associated with the level of health a person possesses. To measure your telomeres is to gain insight into your cellular age, rather than simply your chronological age. In their 2009 study, "Can Meditation Slow the Rate of Cellular Aging," Blackburn and Epel found beneficial effects on telomere length by reducing stress through mediation and mindfulness practices. If you invest in meditation time each day, you are increasing the odds that you will live a healthier life because reduced stress correlates to better health. Tiger Performance Institute has a program that includes a test to understand the telomere profile of a client. We then use that test in conjunction with genetics testing and an array of additional advanced tests to determine the overall health trajectory of that client to then implement habit changes that will positively impact the client's future health and performance every day.

Worth a Try?

Meditation is not a cure-all, but there's certainly sufficient evidence that it provides positive outcomes for those who practice it regularly. Everyone from Anderson Cooper and congressman Tim Ryan, to companies like Google, Apple, and Target are integrating meditation into their schedules, and its benefits seem to be felt after a relatively short amount of practice. Some researchers have cautioned that meditation can lead to ill effects under certain circumstances (known as the "dark night" phenomenon), but for most people—especially if you have a good teacher—meditation is beneficial, rather than harmful. It's certainly worth a shot: If you have a few minutes in the morning or evening (or both), rather than turning on your phone or going online, see what happens if you try quieting your mind, or at least paying attention to your thoughts and letting them go without reacting to them. If the research is right, just a few minutes of meditation a day may make a big difference.

Habit 4: Movement

One Simple Habit to Change Your Life

Thus far you have gained insights into three habits that can reduce interference and improve performance within your life. This fourth habit is going to be more of a challenge. Why? Well, it's simple, but you will have to fight against time and motivation. Making the time for daily movement is a conscious choice you must make to get the most out of your transformation plan.

The Harvard Nurses' Health Study, which has been tracking the health behaviors of more than 200,000 women for more than three decades, has shown the benefits of walking. I'll skip the details, but the bottom line of the study showed that moving for 30 minutes five to six days a week has significant positive effects on your overall health. You can reduce your risk of the major preventable chronic diseases (i.e., type II diabetes, cardiovascular disease, and high blood pressure), you will improve your mood and focus, and you'll improve the neurobiology of your brain.

If you aren't a workout ninja, (I'm not!) it's okay, that's not the point. The Harvard study focused on the impact of brisk walking and almost everyone can walk briskly, no gym required. My recommendation is to first talk to your primary care doctor to make sure that you don't have any restrictions or to understand what yours are before beginning any kind of workout program. Another thing you can do as you begin to exercise is to fill out the Get Active Questionnaire (www.csep.ca). It's the gold standard in pre-exercise assessment by the exercise science and personal training industries, and it's meant to protect you.

Once this is done, start simple and slow. If you're knowledgeable about physical movement and want to create a program or schedule, that's fine. However, if it's been a long time since you've exercised or you're new to it, it's worth hiring a personal trainer to design a program for you to progress safely. If you really lack motivation and have the resources, consider hiring a personal trainer to meet you two or three times a week to push you and keep you accountable.

The biggest key to movement success is simply to start. The hardest part is always getting started. I strongly suggest you make a plan to commit to moving every day of the week, even if it's just for 10 minutes some days. If you're already in the habit of exercising, use brisk walking as a way to stay active but still recover. Building a daily movement habit becomes the key to enhancing your habit formation in other areas. Everyone should be able to make time to walk 30 minutes a day.

Remember, according to University College London research, habits take on average of 66 days to form, not the 21 days that is so often mentioned. In his book *The 5:00AM Club*, Robin Sharma coined this phrase I like to use when establishing a new habit, "It's hard at the beginning, messy in the middle, and beautiful in the end." Just know that movement is a force multiplier: You will get over-sized gains and impact just from this one habit, if consistently applied, and over time, it will be life changing.

The Amazing Things Movement Does to Your Brain

Essentially the purpose of exercise is to stress, stretch, and gently damage the muscles, ligaments, tendons, bones, and arteries at a low level so that when they recover, they rebuild into stronger versions.

Jack LaLanne, America's famous exercise evangelist said, "It's a pain in the glutes, but you gotta do it… I hate working out. Hate it. But I like the results."

I'm not sure I hate exercise because I feel great when I'm done, but I hate the getting-started part. Motivating yourself to literally start is often the hardest part to any workout, however, the positives of consistent activity are so immense that you'd be crazy not to make it part of your day, every day, for the rest of your life.

Consider these facts about physical activity:

- It releases brain derived neurotrophic factor (BDNF), which is like miracle grow for your brain because it enhances neuron growth and learning.
- It catalyzes the release of insulin-like growth factor (IGF-1), vascular endothelial growth factor (VEGF), and fibroblast growth factor (FGF-2), which push through the blood-brain barrier and do some amazing work such as promoting the formation of new neurons, improve insulin sensitivity, and heart function.
- It releases hormones for anabolic growth (testosterone and human growth hormone).
- It releases dopamine and serotonin, which motivate us and elevate feelings of well-being.
- It elevates norepinephrine, which influences attention, perception, motivation, and arousal.
- It helps relieve or lessen anxiety and depression.
- It helps manage cortisol, the hormone of fear.

All of these amazing effects are from movement! When you review this list, aren't you curious as to why more people don't move more often? Sadly, education, purpose, and tools are lacking.

Another important thing to mention is that there's no "one best way to move." Never let anyone put you in a box of "how you're supposed" to exercise. The key to reaping the benefits above is movement that leads you out of "homeostasis," or a comfortable, balanced state. Your body needs some stress in order to work and grow stronger.

Seriously consider what it would take for you to build the lifetime habit of movement into your life in order to change your brain and your overall health profile while also improving your attention, mood, motivation, and overall mental health.

Movement Doesn't Have to Mean Hardcore Exercise

According to Dr. Thomas Frieden, former director of the Centers for Disease Control and Prevention, "Walking and other forms of regular physical activity are the closest thing we have to a wonder drug."

As you begin your movement routine it's important to understand what qualifies as movement in order to create your own program—the one that works best for you—instead of feeling like you're forced into a canned routine.

We all have different levels of fitness, schedules, and interests. Additionally, it's not good for our bodies to do high intensity training seven days a week, however, it's important that we do move every day to optimize our health.

The simplest, cheapest version of movement is something we do every day, often without a second thought—walking! Walking just 2½ hours a week, or 21 minutes a day, can cut your risk of heart disease by 30% and it's also been shown to reduce the risk of diabetes and cancer, lower your blood pressure and cholesterol, and keep you mentally sharp.

It gets better: A University of Utah study found that for every minute of brisk walking women did throughout the day, they lowered their risk of obesity by 5%. So there is absolutely no way you can say you don't have time to move or that it won't help you!

Walking even boosts your mood. Studies confirm it can be as effective as medication for decreasing depression and it can help with everyday stressors by aiding in balancing your autonomic nervous system out of stress-response mode.

Still need help moving? Consider getting a dog. People who have dogs are over 40% more likely to get out and walk, not to mention your levels of social interaction will increase. Owning a dog increases the likelihood that you'll go for a walk and actually talk to other people while walking. Moving and engaging socially with others in conversation is consistent with the findings of a MacArthur Foundation study on longevity. The study demonstrated that a vibrant social life was one of the three key drivers of longevity.

Hopefully by now you are convinced that getting out and walking is too valuable of a habit for you to ignore.

When we refer to health span at Tiger Performance Institute, we are talking about the number of years you are active, healthy, and free of disease and serious physical limitations.

Our research indicates that individuals' personal choices and habits account for over 70% of why they're able to remain healthy and fight illnesses, while our genes play a much smaller role. We may not be able to change our genes, however, we can change how our genes express through exercise and healthy habits.

The best way to change your health span is by your choices. The fact that you're reading this book and considering new habits is a good indicator that you're all for the idea of changing or expanding your health span.

Habit 5: Nutrition

Nutrition Choices and the Impact on Performance and Longevity

Dr. Matthew McNamee, naturopathic MD with a specialty in neuro-endocrinology, is a consulting doctor for Tiger Performance Institute. Dr. Matt is fond of emphasizing to our team that our everyday food choices can be thought of as medicine or poison. Good food choices are beneficial to your body and performance, while poor food choices lead to increased inflammation and oxidative stress.

First, let's talk about oxidative stress. Oxidative stress is an imbalance between free radical production and antioxidant defenses, and it's associated with degenerative diseases such as cancer and cardiovascular disease. Anything that leads to interference, meaning chronic and/or degenerative disease, is going to reduce your performance and longevity.

Here are the drivers of oxidative stress:

- Alcohol consumption.
- Excessive saturated fats (animal fats such as meat and dairy)
- Obesity

How can you improve your oxidative stress biomarkers? By changing your nutrition habits.

Ketone diets (paleo, keto, and Mediterranean) all have solid research that suggests adopting those as a lifestyle will significantly improve your health by reducing oxidative stress and inflammation while driving performance. Even simpler, with similar results, is a concept we will discuss later in the book called Time-Restricted Eating, or TRE.

A few simple steps to lower oxidative stress, after the removal of offending items mentioned above, include adding small amounts of the following to your meal plans and snacks:

- Almonds, cashews, walnuts, pistachios, and various seeds
- Avocados
- Olive oil
- Peanut butter

Additionally, adding fruits and vegetables will help you lower the oxidative stress profile in your biomarkers.

What you eat impacts your longevity, day-to-day health, and how you perform at work, school, or on the field. Sadly, there are many nutrition and "diet" plans out there and it can be frustrating to know what to do. Tiger Performance Institute wants to help you focus on simplicity and execution. You can implement a simple, phased set of changes to how and when you eat because it's very difficult to revolutionize how you eat all at once. With this in mind, let's learn more.

Inflammation and Your Food Choices

Inflammation is an important aspect of age-related health problems. These health problems include cardiovascular disease, type 2 diabetes, hypertension, Alzheimer's, and many forms of cancer.

If you want to age better and be more productive into your later years, then you want to focus on your inflammation levels. One of the best ways to do this is to make better nutrition choices every day. As stated before, what we eat should be viewed as either medicine or something that's adversely impacting our health. This idea was motivational for me as I have made poor food choices my entire life and struggled to change old habits. Now with each meal or snack I ask myself, "Is this medicine or is it going to contribute to making me sick?"

An important concept to learn is how food impacts your glycemic index and glycemic load. Glycemic index is the propensity of a carbohydrate to increase blood glucose levels while the glycemic load is simply the cumulative effect of the volume of carbohydrates.

Our Western nutrition habits are loaded with omega-6 fatty acids from oils (generally not as good at omega-3s) and processed foods, which are higher in carbohydrates and lower in fiber. This combination produces a higher glycemic index and glycemic load and studies show correlations between diets that are high in both glycemic index and load and the body's overall inflammation levels.

So, how do you change this profile of the Western diet? Keep it simple to start by first eliminating the foods that have a high glycemic index in order to lower the glycemic load. In other words, take away the problems first.

This was my approach: I cut out the French fries, processed foods that came in boxes and bags, and 90% of my soft drink consumption. My initial goal was simply to eat foods that were real, such as meat, vegetables, fruits, nuts, and high-quality whole grains. The key was that I didn't try to flip a switch and go for the all-or-nothing mentality. My process was gradual; I spent decades getting to where I am so I didn't change all those habits in just a few months.

As these small changes became routine, I shared with my wife the benefits of eating in a way that lowers inflammation. She jumped on board and created eating plans for keto, paleo, and Mediterranean and even put together a Tiger Performance Institute Pinterest page to help others. We still follow those meal plans today.

Now we eat gluten- and dairy-free with a low processed sugar intake. I follow a 10-hour TRE plan, which means that I have my first cup of bulletproof coffee at 8am and my last bite of food is no later than 6pm each day. To truly follow TRE, you can't put anything in your mouth other than water during the fasting period.

At the time of me writing this, I have been properly on TRE for six weeks. I learned that my coffee intake was violating the process, so I had to start over and the impact has been noticeable. I have more energy on my runs, I'm sleeping better, and for the first time in 20 years, I no longer need acid reflux medication. It's also tightened up my waistline. Overall, I feel better than I have in years.

Your Telomeres and Nutrition

Notice how I'm avoiding the word "diet?" It's an overused word that has negative connotations, because at the end of the day (week, month, and year), you should create eating habits that last a lifetime, not just a short period of time to help you lose weight.

As part of the research for this book and the development of Tiger Performance Institute, I've engaged the expertise of clinicians to form a fuel plan for life. It's one that is part of an overall lifestyle of health to lengthen telomeres, improve your performance today and extend your high performance for years. Sounds like a worthy goal, right?

Tiger Performance Institute's approach to new nutrition habits is starting with where you are today. For 30 days you will keep a log of everything you eat to establish a baseline pattern. From there, you can navigate your way into better choices.

Educating ourselves leads to increased awareness, which leads to us adopting better choices/habits, which ultimately leads to better results. Changing this is very hard, especially when it comes to our nutrition habits, but learning more and knowing your "why" are critical pieces to making real changes happen.

Scientists do have a preferred theory about nutrition and telomere health, and it's branded as the anti-inflammatory Mediterranean diet. This eating program is rich in fruits, vegetables, whole grains, nuts, legumes, olive and canola oil, and herbs, and favors fish and poultry over red meats. A large cross-sectional study from the Harvard School of Public Health on the Mediterranean diet indicates that it can increase telomere health. The study published in the British Medical Journal also found that following a Mediterranean diet was associated with longer telomeres. As a reminder, your telomeres are the protective caps at the ends of your DNA chromosomes, as those caps shorten, the likelihood of disease increases. Maintaining good habits around what you eat can contribute to maintaining your long-term health and sustaining higher level performance.

The 80/20 Principle of Eating

One of the biggest frustrations that many people run into when attempting to improve nutrition habits is the confusion of which habits/choices are best for you. If an eating plan has a name, a book, and brand associated with it, there's a high probability that it's a fad diet. While those diets can certainly work, we encourage you to use caution when buying into a "this is the only way to do it" mindset.

One of the helpful aspects of Tiger Performance Institute's health transformation program we call Optimize, is that at the front end of the program your genetics are screened. This enables the doctor to give you specific direction on nutrition plans so together you can make informed choices based on what will work best for you as well as what's best based on your genetic makeup. You can also do this on your own in conjunction with your doctor if they are current on how to read genetic test panels and integrate that information into a nutrition plan.

Here are four basic nutrition pieces that will help you build a plan that works for your lifestyle and interests:

Avoid Intolerances

If you have sensitivity to gluten, dairy, or find that sugar causes issues, avoid it. This is a tough step, but it can make a big impact.

Total Calorie Intake

This has to do with how much you're eating. Your total calorie intake is based on your age, gender, height, weight, and level of activity during the day, and you should get this from your primary care physician. You could also find help from a licensed dietitian or personal trainer with certifications in nutrition. This is something that you should track daily.

Macronutrient Ratio

The three macronutrients are fats, proteins, and carbohydrates. It's important to find the ratio of each that works for you, as well as the ratio of good to bad fats. Again, talk to your doctor or a registered dietitian about this important ratio. A personal trainer with nutrition certification could also be of assistance.

Micronutrient Intake

These are the key vitamins and minerals that pack a punch in terms of nutritional value, and are often found in fruits, vegetables, and other clean, non-modified foods that are considered "real" foods. Fill your diet with these and the first three rules above take care of themselves.

What You Eat Paints a Picture of Your Future

So far you've learned about inflammation, telomeres, the benefits of clean eating, and a little bit about TRE.

As you read this book, the goal is that your thoughts and motivation will progress to the point where you want to begin to make changes. Don't beat yourself up when you fail because you will fail and that's normal. The key is to change your mindset first. When you believe that food is either medicine or poison and you are choosing to make the best food decisions for the life you want, you will notice how that food starts to become medicine for your life.

Once your mind is set, you must start with tiny micro habits, such as eliminating one food that you know is unhealthy. To form a new habit, you need motivation, ability, and a prompt; think of it as MAP (Motivation + Ability + Prompt). This concept was created by BJ Fogg, PhD, a preeminent researcher on habit formation. Motivation comes from your "why." Why do you want to develop new habits and what will be the necessary motivational fuel to affect significant change in your life? The only way to succeed is to combine a good "why" with good prompts (a reminder system) and to start really small. The smaller your micro habits, the easier it will be to actually create a new habit.

So, give it a try. Give up soda pop, chips, or alcohol for one day and then for two days and see how it helps. You'll gain motivation and resolve as you do one simple thing successfully and then you can build on that to start eating the right foods next.

Habit 6: Hydration

Staying Hydrated is Smart

Your body's organs are comprised of mostly water: your brain is approximately 80% water, your muscles and heart 75%, your blood 83%, your lungs 90%, and your skin 64%—no wonder your body works better when you're properly hydrated! Water is essential to good health, but your individual needs vary. How much water should you drink each day? It's a simple question with no easy answer.

Health Benefits of Water

Water is your body's principal chemical component and depends on it to survive. Every cell, tissue, and organ in your body needs water to work properly. For example, water:

- Gets rid of wastes through urination, perspiration, and bowel movements
- Keeps your body temperature normal
- Lubricates and cushions joints
- Protects sensitive tissues

Lack of water can lead to dehydration, a condition that occurs when you don't have enough water in your body to carry out normal functions. Even mild dehydration can drain your energy and make you tired.

How Much Water Do You Need?

Every day you lose water through your breath, perspiration, urine, and bowel movements. For your body to function properly, you must replenish its water supply by consuming beverages and foods that contain water.

So how much fluid does the average, healthy adult living in a temperate climate need? The National Academies of Sciences, Engineering, and Medicine determined that an adequate daily fluid intake is:

- About 15.5 cups (3.7 liters or 125oz.) of fluids for men
- About 11.5 cups (2.7 liters or 91oz.) of fluids a day for women

These recommendations cover fluids from water, other beverages, and food. About 20% of daily fluid intake usually comes from food and the rest from liquids, which means that in terms of water, this would equate to 100oz. or water for men and 73oz. for women.

What about the Eight-Glasses-a-Day Advice? You've probably heard the advice, "Drink eight 8-ounce glasses of water a day." That's easy to remember and it's a reasonable goal, but not optimal. If you can't remember the numbers above, another easy rule of thumb is to drink half your bodyweight in ounces per day.

Most healthy people can stay hydrated by drinking water and other fluids whenever they feel thirsty, however, others need to make a conscious effort to drink water every hour or so in order to stay hydrated. For some people, fewer than eight glasses a day might be enough, but others may need more based on bodyweight, activity level, amount of perspiration and urination, temperature, etc.

In a 2009 study by Dr. Kathryn Kolasa, Dr. Carolyn Lackey, and Dr. Ann Grandjean, researchers from East Carolina, North Carolina State, and University of Nebraska respectively, formed a consensus among nutrition scientists to provide scientifically-based recommendations to inform consumers about fluid intake and hydration. They include the following:

- Water is essential for life.
- Relying on the perception of thirst does not always guarantee appropriate total water intake.
- Foods and beverages contribute varying amounts of water to the diet.
- Consuming a variety of noncaffeinated and caffeinated beverages including water, milk, tea, coffee, juice, soft drinks, and sport drinks can contribute to meeting the body's water requirement.
- Foods including certain fruits, vegetables, soups, and dairy products can also contribute to meet the body's water requirements.
- Appropriate beverages and food choices for an individual may vary based on energy, nutrient, and water needs, as well as consumer preference.

4 Ways Dehydration Affects Your Brain

Most health-conscious individuals are aware that staying well-hydrated is important for the body's health, but it's also critical for brain function. Research has shown that dehydration has several negative neurological and psychological effects, which should be a big motivation to make proper hydration a daily priority.

1. Dehydration affects your mood.

Several studies have identified a link between dehydration and mood disturbances. In a 2012 study, researchers at the University of Connecticut induced dehydration in healthy young women through either exercise or exercise plus a diuretic and assessed the effects on their mood states. Dehydration was found to result in a measurable increase in "total mood disturbance."

2. Dehydration reduces your cognitive and motor skills.

We all know not to drive under the influence of alcohol, but according to the findings of a 2015 study conducted at Loughborough University, we should also avoid driving dehydrated. Volunteers committed a significantly greater number of errors, such as lane drifting and late braking, during a two-hour driving simulation when they were dehydrated. In fact, their performance was just as poor as that of people who complete similar tests while at the legal limit for blood alcohol content. The likely reason is that dehydration reduces concentration and reaction time.

3. Dehydration makes you more sensitive to pain.

One of the more surprising mental effects of dehydration is increased pain sensitivity, which was discovered in a 2014 study by Japanese researchers. Volunteers immersed an arm in cold water to test their pain sensitivity while having their brains scanned and they reported a lower pain threshold (i.e., they felt pain sooner) when they performed this test in a dehydrated state. These subjective reports were accompanied by increased activity in brain areas involved in the experience of pain.

4. Dehydration affects your memory.

Dehydration has also been found to negatively impact memory. In 2010, researchers at Ohio University measured hydration status in a group of 21 older women and had them complete tests of declarative and working memory. A strong link between hydration status and memory skills was found, with the most dehydrated subjects performing poorest on the tests. This effect was partly mediated by blood pressure.

A 2015 study by David Benton and his colleagues found evidence that being dehydrated by just 2% impairs performance of tasks that require attention, psychomotor and immediate memory and working memory tasks.

Factors that influence water needs

You might need to modify your total fluid intake based on several factors:

- **Exercise.** If you do any activity that makes you sweat, you need to drink extra water to recover the fluids lost through perspiration. It's important to drink water before, during, and after exercise. If exercise is intense and lasts more than an hour, a sports drink can replace minerals in your blood (electrolytes) that are lost through sweat.
- **Environment.** Hot and/or humid weather will make you sweat more and increases your fluid needs. Dehydration also can occur at high altitudes.
- **Overall health.** Your body loses fluids when you have a fever, are vomiting, or have diarrhea. Drink more water or follow your doctor's recommendation to consume rehydration drinks. Other conditions that might require increased fluid intake include bladder infections and urinary tract stones.
- **Pregnancy or breastfeeding.** Women who are pregnant or breastfeeding need additional fluids to stay hydrated. The Office on Women's Health recommends that pregnant women drink about 10 cups (2.4 liters) of fluids daily and women who breastfeed consume about 13 cups (3.1 liters) of fluids a day.

Beyond the Tap: Other Sources of Water

You don't need to rely only on what you drink to meet your fluid needs. What you eat can also provide a significant amount of fluids, too. For example, many fruits and vegetables, such as watermelon and spinach, are almost 100% water by weight.

Many beverages such as milk, juice, and herbal teas are composed mostly of water. Even caffeinated drinks like coffee and soda can contribute to your daily water intake. Water will always be your best bet because it's calorie-free, inexpensive, and readily available.

When it comes to exercise, sports drinks should only be consumed when you're exercising intensely for more than an hour. These drinks help replace electrolytes that are lost through perspiration with sugar that's converted into energy during longer bouts of exercise.

Energy drinks are different than sports drinks. They generally aren't formulated to replace electrolytes and usually contain large amounts of caffeine or other stimulants, sugar, and other additives. It's recommended that you choose natural forms of caffeine, like coffee or tea, over sodas and energy drinks.

The water content ranges based on the food are:

- 90–99% water: Fat-free milk, cantaloupe, strawberries, watermelon, lettuce, cabbage, celery, spinach, pickles, squash (cooked)
- 80–89% water: Fruit juice, yogurt, apples, grapes, oranges, carrots, broccoli (cooked), pears, pineapple
- 70–79% water: Bananas, avocados, cottage cheese, ricotta cheese, potato (baked), corn (cooked), shrimp
- 60–69% water: Pasta, legumes, salmon, ice cream, chicken breast
- 50–59% water: Ground beef, hot dogs, feta cheese, tenderloin steak (cooked)
- 40–49% water: Pizza
- 30–39% water: Cheddar cheese, bagels, bread
- 20–29% water: Pepperoni sausage, cake, biscuits
- 10–19% water: Butter, margarine, raisins
- 1–9% water: Walnuts, peanuts (dry roasted), chocolate chip cookies, crackers, cereals, pretzels, taco shells, peanut butter
- 0% water: Oils, sugars

(Data from the USDA national nutrient database for standard reference, release 21, as provided in Altman.126.)

Staying safely hydrated

Your fluid intake is probably adequate if:

- You rarely feel thirsty
- Your urine is colorless or light yellow

A doctor or registered dietitian can help you determine the amount of water that's right for you.

To prevent dehydration and make sure your body has the fluids it needs, make water your beverage of choice. It's also a good idea to:

- Drink a glass of water or other calorie-free or low-calorie beverage with each meal and between each meal.
- Drink water before, during, and after exercise.
- Drink water if you're feeling hungry. Your body often confuses thirst for hunger.

Although uncommon, it is possible to drink too much water. When your kidneys can't excrete the excess water, the sodium content of your blood is diluted, causing hyponatremia, which can be life-threatening. Athletes, especially if they participate in long or intense workouts or endurance events, are at higher risk of hyponatremia. In general, though, drinking too much water is rare in healthy adults who eat an average American diet.

At the end of the day, the concept is simple: Drink the recommended amount of water daily. I personally struggled with this because I'm generally not a thirsty person, so I fall prey to the trap of thinking I'm fine because I'm not thirsty. To become more accountable for my water intake, I downloaded a simple habit tracker app and now each day, as I take in water, I log it and the gamification motivates me to hit my daily water goal.

If you want to perform at an elite level and do deep work that the market values, top-notch cognitive function is a must. Drinking water is one easy way to make sure you don't inadvertently contribute to brain fog and reduced brain function. Don't allow something as simple as being dehydrated to cause interference and prevent you from achieving elite performance.

Habit 7: Sleep Optimization

Have you ever heard someone say, "I'll sleep when I'm dead"? I used to say this, too, and while it sounds like you're an extra hard worker and it tends to be part of the American culture, it's completely dumb. Sleep deprivation is associated with mental health and mood problems, immune dysfunction, diabetes, cardiovascular disease, and shorter lifespans.

In a 2015 study by Dr. Bruce McEwen from Rockefeller University and Dr.Ilia Karatsoreos from Washington State University, research reveals multiple negative consequences of sleep deprivation and corresponding circadian disruption. Short-term disruptions lead to increased allostatic load (accumulated stress), appetite, caloric intake, inflammation, blood pressure, evening cortisol levels, and sympathetic nervous system tone. Short-term sleep loss also elevates blood glucose and insulin levels. Chronic sleep deprivation and circadian disruption leads to obesity, reduced volume of the temporal lobe, and impaired memory as well as an increase in anxiety, aggression, oxidative stress, free-radical damage, and your risk of Alzheimer's and cognitive decline.

In 2015 Gordon B. Feld, PhD from the University of Tubingen in Tubingen, Germany, conducted a study titled, "Sleep Smart-Optimizing Sleep for Declarative Learning and Memory." The study found sleep is not idle time, but rather an active state during which the brain processes information acquired during the previous day and prepares itself for the demands of the next day. Long-term memory is formed during sleep by a process that strengthens memory traces, reorganizes them, and integrates them into established knowledge networks. These processes not only store previously acquired memories, but also renew the capacity for new learning after sleep. Feld states that improved sleeping conditions clearly have a higher impact on overall productivity over increasing the number of hours at work or at the study table.

There are also multiple studies suggesting that poor sleep precedes Alzheimer's disease. A University of Rochester study on mice showed that while in deep sleep, their brains expanded to have more fluid space between cells and enhanced the clearance of beta amyloid, a protein that accumulates in Alzheimer's disease.

When You're Sleeping Your Body is Working

It's natural to think that when you sleep everything just quiets down, but the truth is that there are many human functions occurring as you sleep. It's during this time that your brain takes out the neuro-trash through the so-called glial lymphatic system, which is defined as the waste clearance pathway. Its role is to clear the rubbish and nourish your entire central nervous system with glucose, fats, proteins, and more. Sleep is also when your body most efficiently heals itself because it's when growth hormone peaks and there is massive cell replication.

Here's a summary of what happens when you sleep:

The Body

- Breathing and pulse slow, giving your heart and lungs a break
- Your muscles repair and grow
- Adrenal glands excrete growth hormones and testosterone to build your immune system

The Brain

- Memory preservation and consolidation as short-term memories transfer into long-term memories
- Toxins produced by neurons are flushed from the brain
- New neural pathways are formed, reinforcing connections between cells
- Remembering how to perform physical tasks, learning, and problem-solving occurs

When you sit back and review this list, which is not exhaustive, you can see why not getting enough sleep can be so damaging to your health. When you choose to sleep less, the processes above aren't happening as they should.

How to Optimize Your Circadian Rhythm

It's not complicated to enhance your circadian rhythm. Here are some simple steps that you can take to improve your rhythm and overall sleep:

Daily Routine

- Go to bed and wake up the same time every day, even on the weekends (at the very least during the work week).
- Plan for a total of eight hours in bed every day.
- Put your electronic devices away one hour before bed and/or watch TV through blue light blocker glasses.
- Strive to not watch TV in bed.
- Consider using a natural sleep aid such as "Power to Sleep" or something similar if you have difficulties getting to sleep or going back to sleep once awakened.
- Practice 5-15 minutes of deep breathing before bed.
- Purchase a Phillips Go Lite BLU Energy Light Therapy Lamp, Rechargeable #HF3429 and use it in the morning for 15-20 minutes a day.

Bedroom Preparation

- The temperature should be below 70°F or use a fan to cool the area.
- Make the room as dark as possible and/or consider eye covers.
- Keep pets and kids out of your bed.

Overall Lifestyle

- Move every day by brisk walking or running for 30 minutes.
- Limit your alcohol intake.
- Stop drinking caffeine by 12pm.
- Limit naps to less than 45 minutes so you don't disrupt your circadian rhythm.
- Avoid eating within 2-3 hours of bedtime.
- Choose a TRE plan of 9-12 hours and be as consistent as you can.
- When you feel stressed, respond with diaphragmic breathing.
- Download F.lux software onto your computer or tablet and enable the "night shift" mode on your iPhone or other devices. F.lux is a tool that removes the blue light from your screen to enable you to view your device without disrupting your sleep cycle.

Final Thoughts on Sleep

I have a dear friend who suffered from sleep deprivation his entire adult life. He routinely fell asleep early in the evening only to wake up at around 2am and unable to sleep the rest of the night. This went on for decades. Today, unfortunately, my friend suffers from dementia and lives in convalescent care. He was a vibrant, entrepreneurial, and generous person who is not the person I once knew.

Select and stick with a specific bedtime every night, stay in bed for eight hours each night so you get at least 6.5 hours of actual sleep each night, try to keep the same waking schedule every day, develop a nightly bedtime routine, avoid blue-light from devices within an hour of bedtime, and avoid fluids and food within two hours of bedtime. If you have a sleep problem, don't ignore it; find out what's wrong and fix it—your life depends on it.

Habit 8: Time Restricted Eating

Philosophically, I've chosen to emphasize TRE over intermittent fasting partially because of the strong science that backs TRE as well as because of its simplicity over intermittent fasting. Intermittent fasting is focused on varying lengths of time you do not eat. TRE is focused on a timing rhythm. As I've delved into the research on intermittent fasting, I have found a myriad of plans, all with supporting claims, and as a busy entrepreneur/leader who wants to implement multiple new habits at once, I put intermittent fasting in the "too hard" pile and chose TRE to suit my personal lifestyle.

Let's start with some basics. When you eat, a lot happens in your body:

1. Depending on what you've eaten, your blood glucose (sugar) levels will rise.
2. Your pancreas produces a hormone called insulin.
3. Insulin tells your cells to fuel up on glucose as your gut breaks down your food.
4. Your body releases hormones like cholecystokinin (CCK) and leptin, which signal when you're full.

However, when you eat a lot of carbs and sugar, ignore your body's "I'm full!" signals, and eat frequently without burning off that energy, your body struggles to keep up. Your pancreas must work overtime to process everything, and anything extra glucose gets stored as fat. Over time, those factors can increase your risk of weight gain, insulin resistance, and diseases like diabetes and cancer. Yikes.

A TRE plan follows the circadian clocks of the organs involved in your digestive process. There are functions that must happen during your daily eating windows and there are critical functions that need to happen during the evening and throughout the night according to a routine rhythm. When you continue eating from early morning until late at night, the processes opposite of digestion fail to occur, leading to problems. When you take a break between meals, your glucose levels remain stable, your insulin levels drop, and your body has a chance to clean up shop, all of which can support major benefits like weight loss and longevity.

Let's summarize three major areas that improve when you follow TRE:

1. Weight management—When fasting, you use up glucose and your body transitions to burning fat, a process called ketosis. This will support better overall weight management and is also good for leveling out blood glucose levels, which improves insulin resistance.
2. Autophagy—This is a cellular waste removal process that happens when you fast, which results in improved cellular efficiency and body functions.
3. Healthy aging—Fasting protects your cardiovascular system and improves blood sugar management and brain cellular performance. Animal studies support antiaging effects of TRE.

Overall, if you can build a daily TRE habit, you should experience improved cognitive function, energy levels, alertness, immune function, and reduce your long-term risk of life-threatening and shortening chronic diseases.

These benefits lead to better day-to-day performance and likely give you more time—for your family, friends, and to advance your goals.

Autophagy: Activate Your Anti-Aging Pathway

It seems like every day there's a new dietary recommendation to adopt with its many health promises, so it's sadly natural if you find yourself jaded, completely confused, and unsure about what's really the best nutrition plan for you.

In many cases, though, the recommendations for dietary selection are associated with weight loss—go on a certain diet and lose a certain amount of weight. But what if we could eat in a certain way to activate our body's best anti-aging system? What if we could find a way of playing with our macronutrients by eating certain foods that truly optimize our health and longevity?

Enter autophagy. Even if you're an avid follower of the health and wellness scene, there is a good chance you might not have heard of autophagy. It wasn't until 2016 when a Nobel Prize in Physiology + Medicine was awarded to Yoshinori Ohsumi for his discoveries of the mechanisms of this biological removal and recycling pathway.

Breaking it down, "auto" means "self," and "phagy" denotes "cell-eating," so autophagy essentially means self-eating in regards to the body recycling its own cells. It's a natural method of cleaning house and is a critical component in maintaining our health at the cellular level by helping to dampen inflammation, slow the aging process, and optimize biological function.

Why is Autophagy Important?

Our cells are constantly being damaged through natural bodily processes such as energy conversion, digestion, and immunity. This happens even in healthy humans and is an important part of the cellular life cycle, which allows the regular generation of new, young cells that can perform optimally in our body.

However, with age, stress, and an increased exposure to foods and chemicals, our cells can experience free radical damage that causes them to be compromised at a faster-than-normal-rate. As a result, the body needs some way of getting rid of these damaged cells. This is where autophagy comes into play. The body employs natural mechanisms to clear out damaged and under-performing cells that linger in the tissues and organs. If these are not removed, they can trigger inflammation and prevent the body from being able to efficiently carry out normal tasks, eventually leading to the development of diseases.

The Benefits of Autophagy

While the body can do this cleanup alone and autophagy are active in all cells, there are many benefits to encouraging regular autophagy:

- Regulates cellular mitochondria, which improves energy production in the body.
- Protects the nervous system and the immune system.
- Protects against metabolic stress.
- Encourages growth of new cells, especially those in the brain and heart tissue, enhancing cognitive function and protecting against heart disease.
- Helps improve digestive function by repairing and restoring the gut lining.
- Helps to protect our genes by maintaining the integrity and stability of our DNA.
- Genetic links have emerged between autophagy defects and cancer, providing increasing support for the concept of autophagy as a bona fide tumor suppressor pathway.

How Fasting + Low Protein Cycling Can Stimulate Autophagy

One great way to encourage this advanced level of autophagy is through the practice of time restricted eating (TRE). This self-digestion not only provides nutrients to maintain vital cellular functions during fasting, but it can also rid the cell of superfluous or damaged organelles, misfolded proteins, and invading micro-organisms. Interestingly, self-digestion by autophagy—a process that is potently triggered by fasting—is now emerging as a central biological pathway that functions to promote health and longevity.

Research shows that 12+ hours of fasting is a great autophagic trigger. When fasting, the levels of glucose in the body are low, which means your insulin levels are. Lowered insulin triggers increased glucagon, the body's natural hormone that can help stabilize blood sugar levels. The presence of this hormone signals the need for autophagy.

How to Do TRE

TRE is elegantly simple: You eat within a shortened period and you fast for the rest of the time. If you're not eating right now, you're fasting, and if you extend your fast a bit longer, you can benefit from it. Potential benefits from fasting include more energy and brain power, and better weight management.

When you follow TRE, you eat within an 8-12-hour time window. Here's what that might look like:

1. Stop your calorie intake (including non-water drinks) by 6pm.
2. Wait until 6am—or 7am or 8am—for your first calories, which includes your coffee.
3. Eat freely, cleanly between 8am and 6pm and try to follow a regular routine.
4. Repeat this schedule the next day.

So, why do people follow TRE? Although weight management is one of the benefits, it's not really a diet. It's an eating schedule that has big payoffs over time, like regulating your insulin levels, protecting against disease, and yes, helping you manage your weight.

This might go against what you've heard about eating frequency in the past, but skipping a meal won't send your body into "starvation mode." Although there's nothing wrong with eating breakfast, there are major benefits to giving your body an extended break between meals.

A quote that reflects this sentiment is, "Health is the crown on the well person's head, only the sick person can see."

You will invest in our health one way or another. The difference is that if you choose now, you can choose how you invest. When you become ill, your choices will likely diminish and the investment required will skyrocket.

Implementation Checklist

✓ Get a physical exam and ask you doctor which of these 8 habits would be most helpful today for you to implement. Alternatively, do a self-assessment and begin on one habit.

✓ Start drinking enough water to hydrate, download a habit tracking app and begin today, it's the easiest habit to start.

✓ Go to www.tigerpi.com and request a free consult. Tiger has options to help you on your elite health journey with supportive coaches and online courses.

Part II:

Psychology of
Performance

"To break through your performance, you've got to breakthrough your psychology."

–JENSON SIAW,
performance coach

The underlying premise of this book, as it relates to getting into the zone, or flow, and doing elite level work is that there are two major components. First, to get into flow, to think deeply, and to develop novel insights that lead to valuable work output, requires great physiology. By that, we mean how your body and brain functions. Secondly, to do great work, it requires a rich and complex combination of psychological factors or you simply won't perform to the level necessary to produce elite-level work.

In Part II you will learn about developing the inner game of performance. The inner game is another way of saying the way in which you manage your internal state of mind. It requires the clarity of knowing what game you are playing, as author W. Timothy Gallwey says in his book *The Inner Game of Work*. Gallwey goes on to say that there is a better game to play, and that game is to play to learn, to play to fulfill your own potential. Ironically, if you do that, you will actually perform better. If you can learn to develop and cultivate a great inner game that uplifts and satisfies you, it will lead to meeting the requirements of whatever outer game (i.e., job, business, or position) you're playing.

I've read a few thousand books in my life and between talking to others and the content of those many books, the subject of performance can range from merely interesting to life-changing. It all depends on your desire to change and to meet the enormous challenges we all face in this next decade alone as our industries, business models, and jobs change rapidly.

Tony Robbins teaches an exercise I really like and have used for years to jumpstart my motivation until I can make enough progress for momentum to kick in. The exercise is to imagine a future scenario where what you want to happen or don't want to happen is reality. In this case, let's imagine technologies are converging to the point where you can see five years into the future and your business model has to undergo radical changes or you're out of business. Think about the emotion of having to shut your business down. What impact will that have on your family? What won't you be able to do for your grand-children in the future because you didn't anticipate and change fast enough? Mediate on this, really feel the emotion, the sensations, and visualize what life would be like without your business.

Now step back, return to now, and realize it was just an exercise. Robbins describes this exercise as getting leverage on yourself. You play out a trend to its logical conclusion, see or understand the conse-quences of not changing, and then use this realization as fuel to start to break through your inertia and make lasting change.

As you go through this book, you will have to do the deep work of introspection. I'm not going to hold your hand by creating a workbook or putting lines in the book for you to write in. I'm challenging you to get a notebook, take notes as you read this section, write down parts that challenge you, and do the work on your inner game.

In this chapter I will introduce key psychological concepts for you to learn and master, then later in the book I will explain how to cultivate and apply these concepts to improve your ability to get in the zone. You can optimize your brain, balance your autonomic nervous system, and have perfect health habits, but if your inner game is poor, you won't live up to your potential. This is the unique point of this book: We have to integrate how our body and brain functions with our inner game to fuel the motivation and mindset to do deep, preeminent work in a vastly changing world.

Chapter 3:

Five Mental Pillars of Elite Performance

The story of Kirk Cousins, quarterback of the Minnesota Vikings, illustrates the major points I want to make in this chapter. Cousins embodies and applies the psychological skills outlined in this chapter, leading to him becoming an established, upper-tier, all-pro quarterback.

Cousins finished high school in West Michigan and was not heavily recruited by the power-five conference schools. In fact, after a waiting game, he received a scholarship offer from only one major school: Michigan State University.

Cousins went to play for Mark Dantonio during the resurgence of the Spartan football program, working his way from red-shirt freshman to starting QB as a sophomore. Cousins went on to finish as the winningest QB in the program's history, setting multiple passing records. When he graduated, he was selected in the fourth round, pick #102 overall, by the Washington Redskins the same year they drafted Quarterback and Heisman trophy winner Robert Griffin III (RG3).

The first three years on the Redskins, Cousins bided his time in a backup role, occasionally getting opportunities to start when RG3 was injured, often struggling with consistency. These were difficult years for Cousins as anyone who has ever pursued a dream and persevered through the lean years knows how the daily battle to overcome negative thoughts and emotions can weigh heavy.

Mindset, belief, grit, and taking responsibility for his results is in Cousin's DNA. Cousins put the time in to understand the game as well as to find experts to help him optimize his body and brain. He had the belief that he could get better and over time he proved that. In 2015, the final year of his rookie contract, coach Jay Gruden named him the starter for the season, making a strong commitment to him at the beginning of the season. Cousins went on to have a great season as a starter. Famously, he then went on to play on two consecutive one-year deals with the Redskins. His goal was to get the contract he believed he deserved or to play for another team, committed to building the future of the team around him.

Today Cousins is one of the highest-paid quarterbacks in the NFL. He consistently delivers strong passing and leadership results and is the franchise QB for the Vikings. He went from the humble beginnings of a lightly recruited high-school quarterback, to beating out a former Heisman trophy winner, to now entering his ninth season as an NFL quarterback. Cousins represents what the psychology of an elite performer looks like.

Growth vs. Fixed Mindset

Dr. Carol Dweck is a preeminent researcher in the area of mindset and how it impacts your outcomes. In her book *Mindset*, Dr. Dweck explains the difference between a growth and fixed mindset and the consequences of each. Her research has shown that the view you adopt for yourself profoundly affects the way you lead your life.

A growth mindset is based on the belief that your basic qualities are things you can cultivate through your efforts, your strategies, and help from others. Although people may differ in many ways (their talents, aptitudes, interests, or temperaments), everyone can change and grow through learning followed by application in order to create hands-on experiences.

When I was in college, I was on scholarship for football. A professor who knew me saw my potential and challenged me to go to the library (remember when we did that?) to read the *Wall Street Journal* every day. I took him up on it most days and it ignited a fire in my belly to learn and grow to prepare for my future in business. From there I began a practice of reading books, newspapers, or magazine articles for 20-30 minutes every day. This ultimately led me to experience three adult careers, start a non-profit organization, and travel to 30 different countries. A growth mindset is not only good for performance, but it also makes for a very interesting life.

The alternative is a fixed mindset. This is the belief that your qualities, talents, and intelligence are carved in stone. Thinking this way creates an urgency to prove yourself over and over, but if you only have a certain amount of whatever it is that you're concerned about, you have to prove it to others or risk feeling inferior or deficient. An example of this thinking is the idea that your IQ score reveals your "whole story." If it's high, you always want people to know that you're smart; if it's low, you place limits on yourself.

A large percentage of people do possess a fixed mindset. Sadly, it was likely conditioned into them by parents, teachers, and bosses who were conditioned to be this way as well. When you're first exposed to Dr. Dweck's research, it's nearly automatic—you want to possess a growth mindset. The good news is that you can cultivate a growth mindset and improve no matter where you are today if you believe you can change and if you believe you are responsible for the outcomes you experience in your life.

The return on investment for possessing a growth mindset has been researched and the evidence is conclusive: Persons with a growth mindset perform better under pressure, they excel in persevering to long-term goal achievement, their engagement at work is stronger, and athletes with a growth mindset perform at a higher level.

To get in the zone and access flow states of consciousness, possessing a growth mindset is a must. One of the triggers you will learn about is the challenge/skills balance, which is the idea that we need to steadily push ourselves and take on challenges that are just above our skillset to experience breakthroughs. If you have a fixed mindset, you have capped out before you've even begun. A fixed mindset person will not make the attempt to push their limits. If it gets too hard, they conclude that they just aren't good enough and quit. A growth mindset person "minds the grind"; they lean in, and because they do, they experience those breakthroughs that lead to flow and huge productivity, creativity, and learning gains.

Internal vs. External Locus of Control

In the last scene of the *El Camino*, the movie sequel to the Netflix series *Breaking Bad*, Jessie is finally free of his past and at peace as he drives up the Alaskan highway to his new life with a new identity. He allows himself to reminisce on a conversation with Jane, the one true love of his life, who tragically died in her sleep after a heavy night of taking drugs. In this final scene, Jessie says to Jane in his rough street vernacular, "I was thinking about that thing you said, about the universe. You know, going where the universe takes you? Right on. I think it's a great philosophy." Jane responds nonchalantly yet forcefully, "I was being metaphorical. It's a terrible philosophy. I've gone where the universe takes me my whole life, and it's better if you make those decisions yourself."

The dialogue in this scene sets the stage for the idea of locus of control, or the idea that the level of control you have in your life is based on how strongly you believe in your own power to control situations and/or experiences that affect your life. This concept is important because if you want to perform at a higher level and thrive in what's sure to be a chaotic decade to come, you need to marshal every psychological advantage you can in order to put yourself in the position to succeed. Establishing an internal locus of control is one of them.

If you have raised children, you understand the concept of locus of control well, if not the term. When faced with the consequences of some negative behavior, children naturally look to blame someone else or the circumstances as to why they did what they did. Parents' jobs are to help children learn to make the connection between their choices, attitudes, and actions and their results and consequences. If a child has not received this sort of guidance, they grow up and enter the workforce and positions of leadership with a tendency to deflect rather than own their results and the consequences of their actions, which makes it difficult for them to learn, grow, and adapt in a positive manner.

Locus of control describes how a person internalizes outcomes. The question is: Does a person believe that her/she, as opposed to external forces (beyond their influence), has control over the outcome of events in his/her life? The theory was developed by Julian B. Rotter, professor and researcher at the University of Connecticut, and has since become an aspect of personality study. A person's "locus" (plural "loci," Latin for "place" or "location") is conceptualized as internal (a belief that one can control one's own life) or external (a belief that life is controlled by outside factors that the person cannot influence, or the idea that chance or fate controls their lives).

Individuals with a strong internal locus of control believe events in their lives derive primarily from their own actions. For example, if a baseball pitcher throws poorly in a game and has an internal locus of control, he'll take ownership of the results. Another pitcher, who also performs poorly, but possesses a strong external locus of control, will place the blame outside himself, potentially onto his teammates, the weather, or the umpires.

Locus of control is connected to the concept of a growth vs. fixed mindset. The important, bottom-line statement is if you want more flow in your life, if you want to get in the zone and do your best work, you need to merge possessing a growth mindset with an internal locus of control.

As a leader, I have had the opportunity to work with thousands of people in my past and current pursuits, and the most challenging person for me to lead was the person with a fixed mindset and the one who possessed an external locust of control. It's difficult to develop momentum with this person because they fail to improve and grow. Their mistakes are viewed negatively, which prevents them from learning from the experience to grow.

On the other hand, the most rewarding relationships are of the parent with children who learn to embody both a growth mindset and cultivate an internal locus of control. As a parent you offer guidance, watch them work through struggles, and celebrate with them when they grow through the challenge to a new level of experience. It's the same with people you lead; as they embrace learning, take risks, make mistakes, and overcome those mistakes, they develop a new capacity to perform and eventually develop into peak performers who lead others.

Finally, to access flow and realize exponential gains in learning, creativity, and productivity, you must embrace the process of struggle, learning, adaption, and change. To do so means internalizing and applying both a growth mindset and possessing an internal locus of control.

Self-efficacy

Related to both mindset and locus of control is self-efficacy, or the role that belief in yourself plays in becoming an elite performer. The pioneer of self-efficacy theory is Albert Bandura, a PhD at Stanford University who developed the initial research on self-efficacy and its impact on human motivation. Bandura invested his entire professional life conducting extensive research developing and building upon his theory of self-efficacy and belief.

Perceived self-efficacy is defined as a person's beliefs about their ability to perform and achieve a result that influences events that affect their lives. Self-efficacy beliefs determine how people feel, think, motivate themselves, and behave. People with confidence in their abilities approach difficult tasks as challenges to be mastered rather than as threats to be avoided. This outlook fosters intrinsic or self-generated interest and deep engagement in the pursuit of goals. This leads to setting challenging goals and maintaining a strong commitment to them. Self-efficacy leads to perseverance and grit to overcome short-term setbacks and failures. Individuals with strong self-efficacy attribute failure to insufficient effort or deficient knowledge and skills that are acquirable, rather than projecting blame outward. They approach threatening situations with assurance that they can exercise control over them. A person with a confident outlook, produces more personal accomplishments and reduces anticipatory stress.

In contrast, people who doubt their abilities shy away from challenges that they view as personal threats. They have low aspirations and weak commitment to the goals they choose to pursue. When faced with difficult tasks, they dwell on their personal deficiencies, on the obstacles they encounter, and all kinds of perceived adverse outcomes rather than concentrate on how to perform at their best. Low self-efficacy leads to reduced effort and causes one to give up quickly in the face of difficulties. Because they have so little belief in their abilities, it does not require more instances of failure for them to lose faith in their ability to achieve the goal.

Bandura's extensive body of research was applied to motivation and learning for both students and teachers. Bandura's research showed that a high perceived self-efficacy led teachers and students to set higher goals and increased the likelihood that they would dedicate themselves to those goals. In an educational setting, self-efficacy refers to a student's or teacher's confidence to participate in certain actions that will help them achieve distinct goals. We can clearly infer from the research that self-efficacy can also be applied to the realm of athletics and individual performance. Bandura's research shows that if we cultivate belief in ourselves, we will set higher, tougher goals and will persevere longer to achieve them.

In Chapter 4 you will learn to apply each of these psychological constructs. Integration of each theory into your character is necessary to get in the zone and perform at a high level. The primary take-away from self-efficacy theory is this: Cultivating a high level of belief in your ability to successfully achieve a goal is critical. If you struggle with belief, the likelihood of enduring through the challenges is low. This leads us to another concept to understand and embody: Grit.

Grit— No Talent Prevails

In the summer of 1982, I arrived at Northwood University as a walk-on football prospect. Although I had talent and a good playing history, I had played at a small, rural high school, which garnered little attention from college recruiters. But I wasn't going to let that stop me.

I reached out to several colleges and found that the coaching staff at Northwood was receptive to me joining as a "preferred" walk-on. I had other opportunities, including one at a larger school, but I believed Northwood was my best opportunity to make the team.

When I arrived, the freshman class consisted of 59 players, which outnumbered the entire number of players on my high school team! I was a bit scared, but I had worked hard all summer and was prepared. The position that I believed would give me the best opportunity to play was wide receiver. However, on the first day of fall camp, I was switched to defense, which forced me to accept reality and adapt quickly—or go home. I was under-weight for the defense position, but I was aggressive and had what I later learned from my coaches was a high football IQ. After just three days of practice, the head coach came up to me and told me that I had performed very well and he would grant me a scholarship to play on the varsity team as the back-up strong safety.

Interestingly, the grind of all-day practices in the heat of summer caused many of the heavily-recruited players to just up and quit. Despite having all of the advantages of size, speed, and accolades, those players seemed to lack the drive to work through adversity, causing them to stop before they ever really started, despite being given a free education by playing at the university. Apparently, talent was no guaranty of success.

I continued to work diligently—I added 30lbs. of muscle, improved my 40-yard dash time, and increased my overall flexibility and athleticism. I also put in extra hours in the film room and studied the opposing team's tendencies. My position required me to know all 11 players' assignments in every situation, which meant moving players around before the snap of the ball when the offense was motioning players to determine what defensive package we were playing.

While I was thrilled that I had managed to make the varsity travel team my freshman year, which is strictly for starters and back-ups along with some of the special team's players, I wanted more. I asked my coaches after my freshman year what I needed to do to start, absorbed their feedback, and went to work. My strengths were that I was aggressive, a good tackler, and I knew where to be at all times and where everyone else needed to be, but I still needed to become stronger and faster.

The planning, strategy, and hard work paid off. I had a passion in high school for football and wanted to play at the collegiate level—and it had become a reality. After my freshman season, I became a starter my sophomore year and ended up starting three seasons of my college career. The significance of starting at a Division II school is minimal, but the life lessons were enormous. I was learning about something researchers would later call grit.

What is Grit?

Angela Duckworth, a PhD researcher at the University of Pennsylvania, has been conducting groundbreaking studies on grit for nearly 20 years. Grit is the quality that enables individuals to work hard and stick to their long-term passions and goals despite hardships and setbacks.

In a 2013 interview with *Educational Leadership*, Duckworth was asked about how resilience and grit were related, which is an important distinction to understand if you want to perform at your best. Duckworth's reply from the article was this:

"The word 'resilience' is used differently by different people. And to add to the confusion, the ways people use it often have a lot of overlap. To give you an example, Martin Seligman, my advisor and now my colleague here at Penn, has a program called the 'Penn Resiliency Program.' It is all about one specific definition of resilience, which is optimism—appraising situations without distorting them, thinking about changes that are possible to make in your life. But I have heard other people use resilience to mean bouncing back from adversity, cognitive or otherwise. And some people use resilience specifically to refer to kids who come from at-risk environments who thrive, nevertheless. What all those definitions of resilience have in common is the idea of a positive response to failure or adversity. Grit is related because part of what it means to be gritty is to be resilient in the face of failure or adversity. But that's not the only trait you need to be gritty."

Duckworth continues:

> "In the scale that we developed in research studies to measure grit, only half of the questions are about responding resiliently to situations of failure and adversity or being a hard worker. The other half of the questionnaire is about having consistent interests—focused passions—over a long time. That does not have anything to do with failure and adversity. It means that you choose to do a particular thing in life and choose to give up a lot of other things in order to do it. And you stick with those interests and goals over the long-term. So, grit is not just having resilience in the face of failure, but also having deep commitments that you remain loyal to over many years."

Professor Duckworth's studies also demonstrate that there is a strong relationship between grit and high achievement. One of the first studies to prove this was her work at West Point Military Academy. West Point produces approximately 25% of the officers in the U.S. Army. Admission to West Point is a difficult process, starting in a potential cadet's junior year of high school. Admission depends heavily on the whole candidate's score, which includes SAT scores, class rank, leadership ability, and physical aptitude. It also requires a Senator's recommendation. Admitted cadets who have successfully gone through the gauntlet of admissions quit at a rate of 1 in 20 during the summer basic training before their first academic year.

Duckworth's interest was in how well grit would predict which cadets would stay. For the study, cadets were required to take a very short questionnaire on grit in the first two or three days of their summer basic training along with all of the other psychological tests that West Point gave them. The results were clear: Of all the variables measured, grit was the best predictor of which cadets would stick around through and after that first difficult summer. In fact, it was a much better predictor than the whole candidate's score, which West Point thought was their best predictor of success at the time.

To borrow a Woody Allen quote from Professor Duckworth's book, "80% of success in life is just showing up." Based on Duckworth's research, grit is one strong factor that determines who shows up. This research has been validated in education, athletics, and business settings as well. Grit ultimately predicts success over and beyond talent. When you consider individuals of equal talent, the grittier ones do better.

In my own collegiate football career, it was my grit, not my talent, that gave me the opportunity to play at that level and receive a free education. As I look back 35 years later, the experience of developing grit consistently showed up again and again in every endeavor I chose to pursue after college.

Gratitude

In a 2015 review of the gratitude research literature, a team of psychologists and neuroscientists in the Netherlands found an inverse relationship between gratitude and symptoms of mental health disorders. High levels of gratitude are predictive of fewer symptoms of mental health conditions and effect motivation, contributing to overall well-being and meaning in life.

The vast majority of research shows that measures of emotional well-being increase in response to a variety of gratitude practices. The research also reveals that gratitude plays a significant role in maintaining healthy relationships as well as in facilitating the formation of new relationships. Gratitude also increases positive behaviors such as helping, sharing, and cooperating, not just toward the recipient, but also toward others in general. The Netherlands' research team suggested that gratitude sets in motion an upward spiral of improved social behavior, reflected by improved emotions, thoughts, and actions that benefit everyone involved.

In a 2017 randomized, controlled study by Australian Professors at Deakin University Sharon Southwell, PhD, and Emma Gould, PhD, participants with a current self-reported diagnosis of an anxiety disorder and/or depression were selected to complete a three-week gratitude diary. Upon returning, participants had lower scores of depression, anxiety, stress, and perceived sleep difficulties, and higher scores of subjective well-being than immediately prior to the study. Authors of the study concluded that gratitude diaries would be a useful intervention technique for distressed populations.

Gratitude is an aspect of your psychology that cannot be ignored if you wish to be a peak performer. The research is vast and consistent that those who practice gratitude have lower stress, improved mood and emotions, and exhibit behaviors that enhance performance. A simple practice to start is every evening before bed, write down three things that happened during the day that you're grateful for. Consistently practicing this daily habit will establish a spirit of gratitude, which will allow you to experience an increased sense of well-being, meaning, and positive emotions that has been confirmed by research.

Implementation Checklist

✓ Go to www.tigerpi.com to find free resources.
✓ Take the assessments for Mindset, Grit, and Internal Locus of Control.
✓ Consider enrolling in Tiger's *Get Into the Zone* online course to deepen your understanding of these five pillars.

Chapter 4:

Fuel for Mental Fire

"Most people aren't anywhere near to realizing their creative potential, in part because they're laboring in environments that impede intrinsic motivation."

—TERESA AMABILE,
PhD professor at Harvard University

My family and I went on a driving vacation this past summer, visiting such places as Door County, Wisconsin; Mt. Rushmore; Yellowstone National Park and Glacier National Park. The hidden gem of the journey was our visit to the Crazy Horse Memorial in the Black Hills of South Dakota, just 17 miles from Mt. Rushmore. The attraction of this memorial is to see the slowly unfolding work of the Ziolkowski family that began in 1948 and continues today. The family's mission is to carve a statue of the famous Oglala Lakota Indian warrior who gained fame for wiping out General Custer and 264 men of the 7th Calvary at the battle of Little Big Horn in 1877.

The project was the vision of a Lakota Elder named Standing Bear. Standing Bear worked tirelessly to find and convince a sculptor to consider creating a monument for this famous Indian warrior. He found Korczak Ziolkowski, a man from Boston who was open to persuasion. In a 1978 interview, just four years before his death, Ziolkowski said to CBS correspondent, Morely Schafer, with tears streaming down his cheeks, "Standing Bear said to me, 'My fellow chiefs and I want the white man to know, red men have their heroes, too.'" At that moment, Ziolkowski was convinced and he made the carving of this memorial for Crazy Horse his life's work. When Ziolkowski moved to South Dakota, he was divorced. He met his future wife Ruth and said to her, "I want you to understand my dear, the mountain is first, and you are second." She accepted this and so have Ziolkowski's children and grandchildren as the work continues today.

In the early years, the project was daunting. Ziolkowski had to erect 731 steps from scratch in a custom manner to traverse the 563-foot mountain, simply to place tools at the summit to begin work on the face. Ziolkowski shared in a video that plays in the visitor center theater that he had a barely-working compressor to power the air tools he needed to jackhammer and drill into the rock. One day, he had to climb the 731 steps nine times as the compressor continued to quit as he worked. But Ziolkowski is a man who would not be denied. He overcame those early obstacles as well as major issues such as funding challenges and even the loss of an excavator machine that his son drove off the mountain and into a ravine. His comment to his son after that incident was, "Son, I'm glad you are okay, but now that you put it there, you go get it."

Now, 72 years later, the statue of Crazy Horse is beginning to emerge. The face is clearly finished, and the work has begun on his arm, which will extend out, pointing ahead as he charges toward enemy forces on his horse. The project will likely take another 50 years and is a prime example for any peak performer to study. Ziolkowski couldn't continually sustain passion for this project unless it came from within. His personal 34-year endeavor on that mountain came from the power of intrinsic motivation and the art of applying grit to a vision that resonated deep within his heart. Three generations of Ziolkowskis have dedicated their lives to finishing the work of their visionary father and grandfather. They are playing the long game at a level few muster the courage to pursue.

As we begin this chapter on the fuel for elite performance psychology, think of Korczak Ziolkowski. Think of his vision—his clear sense of purpose and mission. Think of his goal setting, knowing his personal values and iron-clad work ethic. If you want to enter into the journey of achieving the impossible, it requires sustained motivational and psychological fuel to play the long game through the inevitable crisis of belief that all peak performers face as they climb to the summit of their dreams.

Introduction

How would you like to be so excited thinking about what you're doing that you cannot sit still or stop talking about it? How would you like to possess near-limitless energy? Does having a mindset each morning that's optimistic, hopeful, and positive appeal to you? All of this is possible when you live in an intrinsically motivating way. To live intrinsically, or internally directed, is to be intentional about the things that interest you and that you enjoy. To live intentionally is also to live with extreme clarity—around purpose and your why. Philosopher Friedrich Nietzsche said, "He who has a 'why' to live for can bear almost any how."

Your daily life can be filled with motivation when you consciously integrate principles from the last chapter into your life with specific actions from this chapter. The prior chapter was the theory of performance psychology, and this chapter is how you can implement peak performance psychology to get into the zone and do your greatest work. But I will be blunt: If you read this and take no action, then your ability to do deep, flow work will not happen enough to make a real difference. Integration is the key idea of this book. You must optimize multiple areas of your life, brain, nervous system, body, and psychology to create the foundation for massively transformative performance. I like this quote by author Robin Sharma, "No idea works unless you do the work."

It comes down to this: Will you do the work?

Intrinsic Motivation

If you want to get in the zone—to experience the productivity, creativity, and accelerated learning benefits of flow—you must develop a strong sense of intrinsic motivation. What is intrinsic motivation? It's the motivation to do something for its own sake, for the sheer enjoyment of the task. Extrinsic motivation is the motivation to do something in order to attain an external imposed goal, constraint, or reward.

In a 2015 study conducted by Beth Hennessey of Wellesley College, Seana Moran of MIT, Beth Atringer of MIT, and Teresa Amabile of Harvard found that the development of intrinsic motivation has been linked to creativity of performance, longer lasting learning, and perseverance. The ability to get into a flow state and have intrinsic motivation are strongly linked. In another study by University of Miami professor Seth Schwartz, the increases or decreases in self-determination, the challenge/skills balance, and the ability to break free of social/cultural norms to personally grow were all associated with increases or decreases in interest, flow experiences, and feelings of self-expressiveness.

Separate studies of skateboarders and athletes both revealed that intrinsic motivation drove a richness of experience, improved their performance, and increased the likelihood that their performance goals were achieved. Interestingly, a meta-analysis of 128 studies examining the effects of rewards on intrinsic motivation found that rewards tied to engagement, completion of tasks, and performance all undermined intrinsic motivation. Essentially the study found that any sort of external reward eroded the positive impact of intrinsic motivation. On the other hand, the study showed that positive feedback positively impacted free choice behavior, interest in a task, and intrinsic motivation.

In Daniel Pink's book *Drive: The Surprising Truth About What Motivates Us*, he asserts that the secret to high performance and satisfaction at work, school, and home is the deeply human need to direct our own lives, to learn and create new things, and to do better by ourselves and our world. In *Drive*, Pink identifies three keys to finding your own intrinsic motivation: Purpose, mastery, and autonomy.

With time and intentionality, we can shift from an extrinsic motivation mode of operating (relying on outside forces to help us get going) to an intrinsically motivated life of enjoyment, purpose, and growth. When you're intrinsically motivated, your days are more likely to be filled with curiosity, passion, and fun. To get there, though, we need to do some reflective work and planning. This involves formulating your core values, a transformative purpose or strong "why," and then setting goals in alignment with your values and purpose. Finally, we must execute those changes and goals, and for that, I have provided you with some basics in how to form habits because your habits define your destiny.

Core Values

Your core values define who you are, what you hold dear, what upsets you, and what operates underneath your decisions. Core values essentially state what is important to you. They are a short-hand way of describing your motivations and together with your beliefs, they are the factors that drive your decision-making and behavior.

Core values are something few people take the time to work through to decide what is most important to them, and fewer still actually write them down. Operating without core values is essentially attempting to navigate life with no lens from which to view it through in order to make decisions or choose directions.

Core values are a key aspect of developing powerful intrinsic motivation in your life. Your ability to get in the zone is predicated by you having a high degree of interest in what you are doing. If your core values are absent, you will be unsure of if what you're pursuing is exactly the right fit for you. In author Russ Harris' book *The Confidence Gap*, he states that the mismatch between a person's goals and their values is the primary reason for their lack of confidence. The reason for this is if someone sets goals without considering their values, they may pursue the wrong goals. Harris indicates that his research has revealed that subconsciously our mind will work against goals that are not in accordance with our values. This leads to procrastination, a lack of progress toward certain goals, which then feeds a feeling of inadequacy or a lack of self-confidence.

Core values enable you to live by the principles that are most important to you rather than trying to think from a rules perspective or having no compass. Goals are a destination whereas core values are what you do every day, and to be most effective, you must link the two together. Core values provide the perspective from which you set goals and give you the confidence you've set the right goals in the first place. Taking the time to think through your core values aids in your decision making, which then promotes focus on what you're most interested in, ultimately improving your ability to achieve flow states.

To determine your core values, I recommend an excellent website: www.valuescentre.com/tools-assessments/pva/

This personal values assessment is free and will provide you with a list of words that seem to fit who you are. From that list, I recommend that you take the 10 words you've selected and write a short statement about what each word means to you. After a bit of time reflecting on the words you've chosen, narrow the list down to 5-7 words that really reflect the person you want to be. From these core values you can now set goals that will be congruent with who you are at the deepest level. As you set goals from your core values, your intrinsic motivation will grow because of this alignment.

Purpose

"Purpose is that power that will propel you to get out of bed each morning and push you to make your goals a reality."

—UNKNOWN

Once you have formulated and committed to a set of core values, it's time to decide what your purpose is. Purpose is what gives life meaning. Every action, every word, and every thought should have a purpose. Plato wrote, "Wise men speak because they have something to say; fools because they have to say something."

Setting a goal for ourselves in life and acting toward that goal feeds our sense of intrinsic motivation. "If what you are doing is not moving you toward your goals then it is moving you away from your goals," says Brain Tracy. If your aims are high and purpose is great, your achievements will also be great. Socrates, in Plato's *Apology*, said, "An unexamined life is not worth it." An unexamined, aimless life is led only by animals and those with no goals or direction. On the other hand, someone interested in elite performance must reflect and examine their life and decide to lead a life of purpose.

An exercise that can be helpful in determining your purpose is to ask yourself, "What five things am I most curious about?" Think deeply about this—what areas are you interested in learning about, reading on, and talking to others about? Next, think about five problems that either you have in interest in or that affect you and you want to see solved. From these two questions, find overlap and search there for purpose. Your purpose can be driven by your system of beliefs or worldview, as well. The important thing is to find where you have great belief, great interest, and great passion, and that's where you'll find your purpose.

Your purpose or your "why;" the fuel that enables you to overcome the myriad of obstacles that show up whenever you choose to live intentionally, pursuing a predetermined goal or set of goals. Without purpose, most people give up at the first sign of resistance to their goal. When faced with resistance, someone operating with vision and purpose will push through and get to the next level of progress.

Purpose feeds passion. Passion causes us to do things and make commitments we otherwise wouldn't have made, leading us to people and circumstances we would have otherwise never experienced. Passion drives focus. Focused attention to anything is neurobiologically expensive—it depletes easily. When we have passion, we find focus easily because energy just flows through us as we pursue that passion. Purpose is one of the three foundational drivers of intrinsic motivation, along with mastery and autonomy. To get into the zone, we need intrinsic motivation that comes out of a purpose.

Achievement Through Goal Setting

I remember the first personal development program I ever purchased. It was called *Lead the Field* by Earl Nightingale and it was 12 cassette tapes on different aspects of personal success. My corporate banking career had just begun and I was looking for inspiration and information to advance in my career. The way to do this was not to be the best credit analyst, but to go get new business.

I grew up in a middle-class home in Lansing, Michigan. My dad spent 33 years in manufacturing at General Motors, while my mom stayed home and did an amazing job raising three, strong-willed boys. Because of this background, I had no understanding of sales or how to grow a mindset for successful white-collar knowledge work. I found this program and played these tapes on my way to work in the morning and during the commute home at night for two years, literally wearing them out.

Something that stands out even today, 30 years later, is Earl Nightingale's definition of success. He said, "Success is the progressive realization of a worthy goal or ideal." Nightingale also said, "People with goals succeed because they know where they're going." This catalyzed in me early in my adult life to set goals. Every year since I was in my early 20s, I've set annual goals and pursued them. This developed into more long-term goal planning, which boiled all the way down to daily goals. In Chapter 11 I will share a goal management system that will accelerate your success.

In a 1997 study titled "Effect of Goal Difficulty, Goal Specificity and Duration of Practice Time Intervals on Muscular Endurance Performance," it discussed the effectiveness of goal setting in a sports context. The results of the study indicated that all goal-specific groups performed better than all non-goal-specific groups. In addition, across practice durations, the group establishing difficult goals as opposed to realistic goals exhibited the greatest increase in performance. In other words, difficult or lofty goals are effective with a caveat: If goals are deemed improbable or unattainable, they fail to translate into performance gains.

Edwin Locke and Gary Latham are viewed as the preeminent researchers on goal theory and in their 1980 paper, "Goal Setting and Task Performance 1969-1980," Locke and Latham completed a review of the goal research literature. The results found that in 90% of the studies, specific and challenging goals led to higher performance than easier goals, "do your best" goals, or no goals. Goals affect performance by directing attention, mobilizing effort, increasing persistence, and motivating strategy development.

Locke and Latham's research established that goal setting is most likely to improve performance when the goals are specific and sufficiently challenging, the person has sufficient ability, and feedback is provided to show progress in relation to the goal. Additionally, success and performance increase if extrinsic rewards are present, the manager or those close to the person are supportive, and assigned goals are accepted by the individual. In this research, all goals were assigned, rather than just self-derived ones. From the research on intrinsic motivation, we can safely presume that goals set by the person out of interest and passion will have an even greater impact on performance. The take-away is that the successful person who is seeking to adapt to accelerating technological change must build goal setting into their daily routine and their future planning.

Cultivating Habits to Lean In

Mark Twain said, "A habit cannot be tossed out the window; it must be coaxed down the stairs a step at a time." Elite performers build automation into their lives because doing the impossible—achieving a transformational purpose—is done one step at a time.

The formula is simple:

Clarity of purpose
+
Goals + Habits x Time compounded
=
Exponential results.

Habits automatize your intentions so that you can execute your plans and reach our goals. It has been said that your habits shape your destiny, therefore learning to establish good habits is foundational to getting in the zone and executing on a great vision with success.

In a University College - London study, researchers determined that, on average, it takes about 66 days to establish a new habit. Author Robin Sharma is fond of saying that when you form new habits, it's hard in the beginning, messy in the middle, and gorgeous in the end when you automate a new behavior. American science-fiction author Octavia Butler said, "First forget inspiration. Habit is more dependable. Habit will sustain you whether you're inspired or not." Habits take time to create and they are hard to truly establish, so few are actually able to create new or change old habits.

To change a habit or establish a new one, what must come first: Motivation or action? It's a good question that several researchers and authors have tackled with differing approaches. James Clear, author of *Atomic Habits,* states that if you're having trouble changing your habits, the problem isn't you, the problem is your system. Bad habits repeat themselves again and again not because you don't want to change, but because you have the wrong system for change. You don't rise to the level of your goals; you fall to the level of your systems. This means that you need to create a realistic, practical system to achieve your habit goals. An example would be keeping a journal to track your progress and getting feedback on it. I do this. I have a habit tracker app called "Habit Minder" by Funn Media. I use it daily to help me stay on track—and it's effective and inexpensive to upgrade to full features.

Another view in the motivation vs. action question is B.J. Fogg's work at Stanford on behavioral change. Fogg is author of the book *Tiny Habits* and is an expert on habit formation and behavior change. Fogg's research shows how you can incorporate new habits by starting small—very small. When it comes to change, tiny changes are the key. First, you must identify an existing habit or routine you do every day and anchor the new tiny habit to that existing habit/routine. For example, if you want to begin doing 25 push up per day anchor it to something you do in the morning before you shower. If you make your bed first thing in the morning, start by doing two push-ups right after making your bed but before you head to the bathroom. =The idea is to start small with two pushups—not 20 minutes or two hours. Another example would be taking three deep breaths as your coffee brews in the morning rather than jumping in and trying to do an hour of meditation before work.

The reason for this methodology is Fogg's research on behavior design. He's developed a model for behavior change that's as follows: Behavior = Motivation + Ability + Prompt. You want to start where the ability is easy, but you need a prompt to help remember to actually do that habit so motivation isn't as big of a factor when you start.

An example would be establishing a block of focus time each day to do high-value work. Don't just schedule a full two-hour block of time in the morning right away; you won't be successful that way because the motivation required to make that big leap is too much. Instead, start with 15-minute blocks of time. Put a reminder on your calendar for "15 minutes of focus" and stick to it. It's easier to focus for a short period of time so your ability to complete it shouldn't be a question. Pick one that thing you want to focus on each day and do it every day for several weeks until it's automatic. As this 15-minute focus habit becomes automatic, the motivation to do it is also more automatic and you can now add more time to the focus block. The key is the easier it is to start, the more likely you will do it and continue it. Doing the actual task frequently/every day is more important than what or how much you do it initially. You must gain momentum first, then optimize the habit and repeat the process.

I have been able to implement 23 micro-habits are helping me build up to the bigger things I want to accomplish. For example, I know that in order to get in the zone by accessing flow, I need to be physically fit. To be physically fit, I need to move daily, and through the compounding effects of consistent exercise, I gain the energy and cognitive optimization I need to get in the zone and sustain energy day in and day out. Thus, my training minutes and other movements are tracked daily using my habit app.

Leadership expert and prolific author John Maxwell says, "You'll never change your life until you change something you do daily. The secret of your success is found in your daily routine." A good daily routine, stacked with good habits, executed day in and day out over months and years is how all the greatest performers show up. To gain the benefits of physical and mental optimization outlined so far in this book, you have to execute using powerful habits. When you do, you set yourself up to enter the zone.

Implementation Checklist

✓ Take the core values assessment.
✓ Develop 5-7 core values that define who you are.
✓ Develop a transformative purpose.
✓ Pick one habit to develop now and see it through the 66-day average time it takes to make it stick.

Part III:

Flow and Elite Performance

"It is when we act freely, for the sake of the action itself rather than for ulterior motives, that we learn to become more than what we were. When we choose a goal and invest ourselves in it to the limits of concentration, whatever we do will be enjoyable. And once we have tasted this joy, we will redouble our efforts to taste it again. This is the way the self grows."

—MIHALY CSIKSZENTMIHALYI,
author of Flow: The Psychology of Optimal Experience

I made the assertion in the introduction that we are living in a period that MIT Professors Erik Brynjolfsson and Andrew MacAfee have dubbed the Great Restructuring. We are living in a time where 12 major technologies are accelerating their tech improvements and adaptations and converging into novel solutions for a myriad of problems. This acceleration and convergence will change our business models, rendering many obsolete, and eliminate millions of jobs in their current form.

The case to be made is that in anticipation of the pace of change we face, we will have to feel our best and work our best to positively adapt through the next 10 years of the 2020s. Again, this is a period that technologists believe 100 years of change will occur in a single decade, causing unprecedented disruption to industry and peoples' lives. If you can be one of the ones who make this transition positively, enormous opportunities await those who can bring accelerated learning, elevated focus, and elite performance to the task.

The answer is not to squeeze harder, or to push for just a few more hours a week, or to optimize our schedule a little bit and improve incrementally. What's required is a transformation of how you operate—cognitively, physically, psychologically, and how you design your life to meet this challenge. The answer is flow; to get into an optimal state where you feel your best and work your best, every day, day after day. My goal is not to simply survive, but also to accelerate my achievement, performance, and success in the face of immense change.

Chapter 5:

Now Entering The Zone of High Performance

In his autobiography, *Second Wind*, former NBA Celtics' Hall of Fame star Bill Russell writes, "It was almost as if we were playing in slow motion. During those spells I could almost sense how the next play would develop and where the next shot would be taken." This tunnel-vision phenomenon is reported by athletes, creatives, and psychologists alike as a hyper-focused, sometimes spiritual, state of mind where anything is possible. It's where we become our most productive, creative, and powerful selves. The argument of this book is that in order to adapt to the incredible amount of technological change, we need to learn new things quickly and sustain elite levels of performance. Getting in the zone or flow is the answer, not working harder or longer.

In the next three chapters I will explain what flow, or getting in the zone, actually is as well as what the building blocks for flow are and how to cycle through flow in order to get in the zone repeatedly. When you're able to get in the zone at will, you can enjoy the phenomenal payoff in terms of productivity, accelerated learning, creativity, and motivation that comes from flow.

What is Flow?

In her Washington Post article, "It's great to be 'in the zone'—while working, exercising, and creating art," Jessica Wapner described her own experience with flow as a runner:

"By mile 10 of my first half marathon, the persistent, frigid drizzle had forced my fingers into a clenched 'C' shape. The thrill of running alongside thousands of people after weeks of solo training had mellowed into a quiet, somewhat dull drive toward the finish line. Then, without warning or conscious effort, my body started moving faster. The hard pavement felt like a supportive mattress. A sense of elegance freed me from my clumsy body. I was—there is no other way to put it—at one with the cityscape around me. I was in the zone."

As a relatively new runner myself, I have had the same experience. A little context first—I was a sprinter on the track team in high school, and throughout my collegiate football career my entire focus was on improving speed and quickness, not endurance. After many years of doing little to no consistent running, I began seriously training about a year ago for endurance running, more so to be fit than to set any race records. On a recent run I had the same experience as Wapner. At the nine-mile mark of a 10.5-mile run, I experienced the sensation of being pulled forward, my legs were driving harder, pain subsided, my mind cleared, and I ran faster the last mile than the prior nine, and like Wapner, I was clearly in the zone.

What is getting in the zone/flow? The terms are used interchangeably with most people recognizing and understanding the term "zone" better than "flow." Irrespective of the terms, flow or getting in the zone is a proven state of consciousness and the key to achieving elite levels of performance in the future.

F.G. DeKock, a PhD professor at the University of South Africa, offers a simple definition of flow that will build until you have a solid understanding of what the term means. DeKock says, "Flow is a mental state characterized by a feeling of energized focus, complete involvement, and success when fully immersed in an activity."

The "Godfather of Flow," Mihaly Csikszentmihalyi describes flow in his book, *Flow and the Foundations of Positive Psychology: The Collected Works of Mihaly Csikszentmihalyi*, as "the holistic sensation present when we act with total involvement. It is the kind of feeling after which one nostalgically says: 'that was fun,' or 'that was enjoyable.' It is the state in which action follows upon action according to an internal logic which seems to need no conscious intervention on our part. We experience it as a unified flowing from one moment to the next, in which we feel in control of our actions, and in which there is little distinction between self and environment; between stimulus and response; or between past, present, and future." In its simplest terms, Csikszentmihalyi describes flow as an optimal experience.

Robert M. Nideffer in his article, "Getting into The Optimal Performance State," Which was published in *Enhanced Performance Systems,* describes the flow state "an optimal performance." He defines flow as a state whereby a person, on a relatively infrequent basis, feels totally immersed in the performance. When that happens, according to Nideffer, performers describe the experience as something outside of the ordinary. They are "in the moment," performing at an automatic level, without need for conscious thought and direction. They feel totally in control, completely focused on the task, extremely confident with a total loss of self-consciousness, and their perception of the passage of time is altered, either losing all awareness of time or feeling as if things are happening in slow motion.

In Herb Benson and William Proctor's book, *The Breakout Principle: How to Activate the Natural Trigger That Maximizes Creativity, Athletic Performance, Productivity, and Personal Well-Being,* they define flow as the breakout principle. The breakout principle is, "a powerful mind-body impulse that severs prior mental patterns and even in times of great stress or emotional trauma, opens an inner door to a host of personal benefits, including greater mental acuity, enhanced creativity, increased productivity, maximal athletic performance, and spiritual development." The book asserts that you can learn this as a skill and turn off prior mental patterns and activate breakouts at will, which will transform your life.

The zone is a state of heightened performance and enhanced decision making, in fact decisions become almost automatic. Your inner critic or voice of doubt goes quiet, removing some of the self-imposed limits on your thinking. Your creativity and pattern recognition improves, leading to more effective problem solving.

Historically, the belief was that flow originated in the pre-frontal cortex (PFC). It's where you collect data, problem solve, plan ahead, make risk calculations, analyze information, manage impulses, learn from experience, and make character-based decisions. Thus the belief that the PFC catalyzes flow is logical since it's the center of your higher cognition.

Arne Dietrich, Professor of Cognitive Neuroscience, American University, Beirut says,

"The prefrontal cortex is where thinking happens," he explains. "It's where we take simple ideas and add all kinds of layers of complexity to them. But I was slipping into flow of a regular basis and always amazed by the clarity of the state. All that complexity was gone. Decisions were easy and automatic. It was like the opposite of thinking."

Dietrich's research led him to discover how the brain was eliminating this complexity and it led him to understand that the brain wasn't eliminating complexity, it was eliminating the very structures that created this complexity. "We had it backward," he says. "In flow, parts of the PFC aren't becoming hyperactive; parts of it are temporarily deactivating. It's an efficiency exchange. We're trading energy usually used for higher cognitive functions for heightened attention and awareness." This efficiency exchange is called transient hypo frontality. Hypo means slow as opposed to being hyper, which is fast.

So, the success teachers of the past propagated a myth that if you could use even just 10% of your brain, enormous success awaited right around the corner. The success industry preached that you had to learn more and work more diligently in order to use more of your brain. The reality is that they had it wrong; you need to use less of your brain and this is what getting in the zone is all about. In fact, to get in the zone, you need to do less as well and this is the paradoxical challenge to over-achieving type-As who struggle with less-is-more thinking.

Now that flow has been defined, let's examine what flow looks like more systematically. Through a series of extensive research studies across various activities (i.e., chess, rock climbing, dance, arts, and work), Csikszentmihalyi and colleagues identified nine major components of flow experience:

1. Challenge-Skill Balance—A sense that one is engaged in a challenge equal to one's current ability.
2. Action-Awareness Merging—Involvement is so deep that action feels spontaneous and almost automatic.
3. Clear Goals—A feeling of certainty about what one is going to do.
4. Unambiguous Feedback—Immediate and clear feedback about one's action.
5. Concentration on the Task at Hand—A feeling of being intensely focused on what one is doing in the present moment.
6. Sense of Control—A sense that one can deal with the situation because one knows how to respond to whatever happens next.
7. Loss of Self-Consciousness—The inner critic, the voice of doubt turns off.
8. Transformation of Time—A sense that the way time passes is distorted.
9. Autotelic Experience—The experience of the activity as intrinsically rewarding.

From this list you can see that many of the principles already explained in this book come into play. Flow is a neurological fact, validated in research. It's a complex state that comes from the integration of multiple disciplines. Getting in the zone is something you can learn. Flow follows focus, and so much of learning flow is learning to train your attention and manage your focus. I believe that focus management, not time management, is the key skill for today's current environment. Once you learn how to achieve flow, you can enter that state at will, provided you also build the foundation for flow into all aspects of your life.

Many of the older ideas about performance and the brain were wrong. Earlier, I referred to that audio course I listened to, which was created by Earl Nightingale. In that course, he propagated a myth believed by many that humans only used a small portion of their brain's capacity. He believed that if you could just focus your efforts and learn more, you would use more of your brain's potential and therefore your fortunes would improve as you used more of your brain. Turns out, just the opposite is true.

When you get in the zone you are actually using less of your brain! It's an efficiency exchange—you need focus, so part of your brain shuts down. It's called Transient Hypo Frontality, which ultimately means temporary lower pre-frontal cortex activity. In the pre-frontal cortex resides our time perception, conscious thought, and executive functions. When you're in flow, this part of the brain shuts down, which explains why time flies by and you have only one thought: the task at hand. You literally get out of your own way when you're in flow, thus when you're working on a task in your area of expertise, honed through the growth process of the challenge/skills ratio, you get exceptional results.

Finally, not only does flow enhance performance, it also promotes meaning and personal well-being. Csikszentmihalyi says, "It stands to reason if you are pursuing goals that are your own and you experience these characteristics of flow on a regular basis, your life will be rich with excitement, growth, learning and progress." Csikszentmihalyi continues, "The unrelated goals of the separate flow activities merge into an all-encompassing set of challenges that gives purpose to everything a person does. When somebody's life is rich in vital engagement their entire existence can become like a unified flow experience."

History of Performance Research

Prior to the 1870s, optimal states and religion were comfortably linked. Interestingly, the teachings of scripture in the Judeo-Christian worldview align with the life pattern and mindset necessary to experience flow. This link between flow and faith began to change with the arrival of Friedrich Nietzsche. Nietzsche was a German philosopher and cultural critic who published prolifically in the 1870s and 1880s. He is famous for uncompromising criticisms of traditional European morality and religion. Many of these criticisms rely on psychological diagnoses that expose, according to Nietzsche, false consciousness infecting people's received ideas. For that reason, he is often associated with a group of late modern thinkers (including Marx and Freud) who advanced a "hermeneutics of suspicion" against traditional values. For purposes of this book, discussion of Nietzsche's ideas will be limited to his concept of "will to power" to explain the historical context of modern thinking on performance and flow.

Nietzsche is quoted as saying, "We are our own kind of chaos." He believed man was a mess and that survival was good, but there had to be more. Out of this, Nietzsche developed the concept of "will to power" as a means to living a life of meaning. Nietzsche explains aspects of human behavior in terms of a desire for domination or mastery over others, oneself, or the environment. The will to power, as Nietzsche conceives of it, is neither good nor bad, it's a basic drive found in everyone, but one that expresses itself in a variety of ways. The philosopher and the scientist direct their will to power into a will to truth, while artists channel it into a will to create, and businessmen satisfy it through the creation of their business vision as their art form.

Nietzsche formed four foundational ideas that underpin performance.

1. You Need an Organizing Idea

To perform well, you need a purpose to overcome yourself. Passion and purpose enable you to overcome your lesser instincts and propel you toward productive activities.

2. Creativity/Self-Expression as an Antidote to Nihilism

Nietzsche was an atheist who spoke against the common morals, values, and traditions. Since God was dead, according to Nietzsche, there was no meaning in religion or faith, so man had to create meaning. I am not in the Nietzsche camp; I believe that you can possess great purpose and passion and still live with values rooted in faith. The point here is that Nietzsche believed innovation and self-expression were part of the performance process.

3. Suffering is Not Optional for Peak Performance

Life can be boring and monotonous if you allow it. It's easier to do nothing. However, if life is going to be dull, choose the hero's journey and take on something big and choose to live with purpose. When you seek performance, you are seeking challenges, and with challenges come suffering. Grit is not optional; to perform is to choose to suffer. Only you get to choose your suffering.

4. High Performance is Not for Everyone

Nietzsche believed that only 10% of the public was cut out for living a high-performance life, while 90% constituted the herd, the crowd, and the drifters living without purpose or passion. He labeled this the "last man" who succumbs to short-term pleasures, who believes in fate and has an external locus of control.

After Nietzsche, Wilhelm Wundt furthered the research on peak performance in the late 1880s and early 1900s by being the first to make the connection between physiology and flow. Wundt initiated the idea of there being a "sweet spot" of attention. He considered attention and the control of attention as an excellent example of the desirable combination of experimental psychological and neurophysiological research. Due to his research, Wundt is considered a forerunner of modern neuropsychology.

In 1908, psychologists Robert M. Yerkes and John Dillingham Dodson developed the Yerkes–Dodson law. Through their research they were able to establish an empirical relationship between arousal and performance. Their law dictates that performance increases with physiological or mental arousal, but only up to a point. When levels of arousal become too high, performance decreases. The process is often illustrated graphically as a bell-shaped curve that increases and then decreases with higher levels of arousal.

Research has found that different tasks require different levels of arousal for optimal performance. For example, difficult or intellectually demanding tasks may require a lower level of arousal to facilitate concentration, whereas tasks demanding stamina or persistence may be performed better with higher levels of arousal to increase motivation.

In the early 20th century, William James became known as the father of American psychology. Early in his life he was confused as to what he wanted and fell into depression. In a turn of inspiration, James decided to embrace free will and switched to an internal locust of control. He immediately felt better and began to live up to his potential. With respect to the idea of potential, James agreed with Nietzsche that most men never live up to what they are capable of, and he put forth habits and attention as the greatest levers that you have in becoming a peak performer. According to James:

1. Sow an action, reap a habit.
2. Sow a habit, reap a character.
3. Sow a character, reap a destiny.

In addition to habits, James believed parental conditioning and culture weigh heavily at a sub-conscious level and can work for or against performance.

James also embraced the need for suffering in order to achieve breakthroughs that led to higher performance. In addition to habits and attention, James believed that optimism, gratitude, fitness, and perseverance were important ingredients in realizing your potential.

In the 1960s, psychologist Abraham Maslow became the first academic to write about what he called "peak experiences," or moments of elation that come from pushing yourself in challenging tasks. Maslow found successful people were interested in success and he believed that people found a way to shift into peak experiences to drive their success. By accessing frequent peak experiences, you self-actualized and created a life of meaning.

Psychologist Mihaly Csikszentmihalyi called it "flow," and his extensive studies, beginning in the late 1960s, eventually drawing interest from researchers around the world. Psychologists have since amassed a wealth of data and insights on flow in regards to what it is, how it works, and why it matters. The purpose of walking you through the history of flow research is to give you confidence in the rigor of flow science. You can trust the science that flow is an actual state and it's empirically supported with performance-enhancing results that can only be called remarkable.

The research has created a road map for all people who want to do deep, high-value, preeminent work—the work of artists, elite athletes, entrepreneurs, chess players, rock climbers, etc., who seek the exhilaration of being completely absorbed in the pursuit of something difficult.

The map begins in the next chapter. Flow has requirements—it has tasks you will want to avoid and others you will want to pursue. Flow also requires that you cognitively forget that you are trying to get there.

Implementation Checklist

✓ Do an honest assessment of how often and how long you experience flow in your daily life over an average week.

✓ Make a list of the things that prevent you from applying total concentration to a task such as a mental health condition, how you manage time, interruptions, or addiction to tech.

Chapter 6:

The Inner Game of Flow

"People who learn to control inner experience will be able to determine the quality of their lives, which is as close as any of us can come to being happy."

—MIHALY CSIKSZENTMIHALYI, Ph.D,
Professor, Claremont Graduate University

It was my pleasure to work with Patrick Chambers, head coach of the Penn State University men's basketball team this past year. Coach Chambers is a dynamic leader with an intense and gregarious personality fitting of a Philadelphia native. He is a former collegiate basketball player himself, a point guard under Hall of Fame coach Herb Magee, who is called the "shot doctor."

Chambers turned his love of basketball into a passion for coaching after a few years in the private sector. He worked his way up to assistant coach at the storied Villanova program under legendary coach Jay Wright. Chambers was there for five seasons, including five NCAA tournament appearances and a Final Four appearance in 2009. Chambers earned the opportunity to become a Division I head basketball coach at Boston University for the 2009-10 season, and during his first year he led the team to a 21-14 record. In his second season, the team finished with an identical record, receiving a bid to the NCAA tournament. Chambers parlayed this record in favor of an opportunity to become the head men's basketball coach at Penn State University, which had a collective losing record over 16 seasons.

When I met Coach Chambers, he was entering his ninth season at Penn State. He had provided strong leadership to the program, but was not yet able to achieve some of the goals he had for the program, such as a winning record in the Big Ten and a post-season appearance in the NCAA tournament. Chambers had identified and shared with me the issues that kept him from entering the zone as a coach to provide insightful and meaningful leadership to his players when it counted during games. These challenges were his interference, the factors that blocked him from the level of performance he was capable of achieving.

Our Tiger Performance Institute team started small so Chambers could utilize some of the performance- and health-enhancing tools we deploy to reduce his interference, which enabled his high-level skills and expertise to take over. The results were impressive. Chambers shared this with me about his experience with Tiger Performance Institute: "As a coach, the primary benefit to me has been that I'm processing and am not as quick to react emotionally. I am more mindful than I have ever been, including parenting and in my relationship with my wife. I like to think my responses are more intelligent and impactful. I think the poise, the calm, and being level-headed was critical to our team's success this year."

Flow gets results. Coach Chambers, through reduced interference, was able to develop personal flow, which led to team flow. As he was able to get into the zone personally, it enabled his Penn State players to play with greater calm and poise, thanks to reduced interference from Chambers. This also enabled the Penn State team to feel and perform at their best. The 2019-20 team finished with the highest AP poll ranking in program history, a winning Big Ten conference record, and for the first time in Coach Chambers' tenure, an expected NCAA tournament bid for March Madness 2020, had it not been for the coronavirus pandemic and subsequent cancellation of March Madness.

The Performance Formula

We at Tiger Performance Institute use The Performance Formula to explain the work we do with clients. The Performance Formula is:

Performance = Skill—Interference

First, the credit for this formula goes to Dr. Anthony Avellino, MD, the Chief Medical Officer on Michigan State University's health team. I was in a meeting with Dr. Avellino describing the work I do, and he pointed to a presentation that he had on his computer with the formula above. I liked it so much that I asked his permission to use it when I explained my work for this book.

Timothy Gallwey, author of *The Inner Game of Tennis* and a series of books on the topic, utilized a similar performance formula. We use "skill" in The Performance Formula because it's a more specific term and reflective of the reality that when you rid yourself of limitations, your skills are what propel your performance.

The key term is "interference." Interference is anything in your life—mentally, physically, or habits/actions-wise—that prevents you or interferes with you feeling your best and working at your best. Interference can be ADHD, anxiety, or another form of a mental health challenge. Interference can include stress, emotional control, or a lack of resiliency. The central idea of the formula is to point out that we all have interference and whatever it is, it works against our performance. When you reduce or eliminate the interference, your skills dominate and your performance accelerates.

The goal of this chapter is to communicate that getting in the zone is something you can engineer into your life. It's a skill and a lifestyle that can be learned and it's accessible for everyone, not just the best of the best. It's a strategy that you can employ to differentiate yourself in your career and to accelerate progress toward your career goals. If you're an athlete, getting in the zone can be learned and used to improve performance during games. Entrepreneurs looking to accelerate the growth of their companies can use flow to overcome the limits of traditional productivity tools to get more done in less time. Flow can be used to simply improve the meaning of your life and the quality of your day-to-day experiences. Getting in the zone is not an elusive idea, it's a concrete approach to elite performance and well-being that you can deploy to accelerate the achievement of your goals.

Flow Blockers

The essence of flow is to achieve complete concentration on a task in an area of interest or expertise whereby your subconscious takes over and the task becomes effortless and automatic and the output is superb. As you make changes that enable you to get in the zone, you will get into the zone more. Later in the chapter I detail what triggers flow and you will learn that it's important to have interests outside of work that you can get into flow by doing. The flow triggers and activities outside of work both support the idea of the more you get into flow, the more flow you get. There is also a cycle to flow that I will explain in Chapter 7 that requires a struggle phase, followed by a release phase, then you are in flow, ending in a recovery phase. Yes, struggle is part of learning to get in the zone.

Now that you understand that flow is essentially attention and we can best apply this attention in situations that are of interest or in our area of expertise, it's time to discuss what prevents us from getting in the zone.

Physiology

Multiple studies have documented the state of our physiology is correlated to our ability to get into flow states. Physiological interference is different for everyone but includes sleep quality and quantity problems, poor heart rate variability, poor nutrition, lack of hydration, and a general lack of fitness. Getting in the zone is a cycle that's taxing; best-selling author Steven Kotler likes to say, "flow is biologically expensive." Stefen Engeser, professor from the University of Trier in Germany and editor of *Advances in Flow Research*, states, "The research is clear, you are much less likely to experience a state of flow when you are in an energetic state of depletion that prevents strong engagement (including highly focused concentration) in an activity." Thus, exhaustion, fatigue, or allostatic load inhibits your readiness to enter a state of flow. Moreover, the state of your physiology affects the length of time you're able to remain in a state of flow as well. When a person systematically optimizes their cognitive function, nervous system, and physical well-being, they build a powerful foundation for experiencing flow on a daily basis.

The idea that the state of your physiology has a direct bearing on getting in the zone highlights the necessity to optimize your autonomic nervous system (ANS) through heart-rate variability (HRV). In flow, HRV decreases due to the load that flow places on the body from a biological standpoint. If HRV is poor, it negatively impacts your ability to sustain concentration to get into and remain in the zone. Another way to improve physiology is to improve brain function through mindfulness practices. An excellent way to accelerate cognitive function improvement, train attention skills, and eliminate interference is through neurofeedback. Electrical signals through the various brain wave frequencies can become dysregulated, causing interference. Excess high frequency beta brain waves increase internal dialogue and anxiousness, and excess theta waves work against focused attention. By utilizing neurofeedback, your brain learns to re-regulate these waves into optimal ranges with repetitive training. Consistent breath work and other strategies to improve HRV can help make brain training gains permanent and set you up to achieve a flow state. Finally, any health imbalances such as chronic disease, poor sleep, and/or poor fitness all negatively impact your ability to get into and stay in flow.

If you want to develop a high-flow lifestyle, both in activities outside of work and to amplify your work, I encourage you to closely re-read Chapters 1-2 and develop a plan to address the areas that you need to improve in physiologically. This is work; you can't expect to exert the effort of taking a pill every day to change your physiology. If you want the top-5% results, then you have to be willing to do what 95% of people are unwilling to do. For many, doing it on their own is not going to get the results they want so they seek a coach to help them. At the end of this book, you will learn about the programs and services that Tiger Performance Institute offers and you should consider partnering with us to help you implement new training and habits that will enable you to consistently live a high-flow lifestyle.

Psychology

Your inner world is a deep well, requiring much reflection, self-awareness, and intentional action to change to enable you to perform better. Your inner world is also a great source of interference, preventing you from getting in the zone. There are situational influences on your psychology and what I call mental characteristics that act as interference in your quest to get in the zone.

Situational influences start with inner ruminations. A person who has a strong pattern of self-talk, negative perceptions, or loud inner critic will have a hard time getting into flow. Fear-based thinking in the face of adversity will prevent flow. Worry about what might or might not happen regarding the future places you in stress response and blocks flow. Loss of autonomy, leading to a loss of interest or motivation, prevents you from getting in the zone. Ultimately being self-aware of the level of these situations and learning to get past them is important in your path to living a high-flow lifestyle.

Mental characteristics consist of limiting patterns of thoughts. If you have a fixed mindset (belief that your skills, talents, and intelligence are carved in stone or fixed), then you will not make the attempt required for the struggle phase of the flow cycle. Flow follows training, hard work, and expertise that has disciplined you to train your attention to gain excellence. Only a growth mindset will embrace going on a path to mastery in a hobby, career, or in the development of a specific set of skills for business or leadership. The struggle phase is foundational to flow that you don't block it by not embracing the learning and growth process.

Additionally, and related to a growth mindset, is owning your results (i.e., an internal locus of control). If you project blame outward as you receive constructive feedback, it hijacks your ability to gain expertise and grow through the struggle phase. Belief also plays a role in blocking flow. If you feel that you're not up to the task, that it's too hard, or believe you lack the skills, then flow will be difficult to achieve. Finally, a lack of grit or ability to lean in and face adversity with perseverance is a surefire way to block flow. Purpose, passion, curiosity, and high levels of interest in what you are doing are your counterweights to these flow blockers.

Stress

According to a 2014 study by the American Stress Association (who knew there was such an organization!), 77% of those surveyed experienced stress to such an extent that they had physical symptoms. Another 73% said that they suffered psychological symptoms and 33% said that they faced severe stress. These numbers are staggering and point to the fact that we are living in an era where stress is epidemic as well as poorly managed.

You recall from earlier in the book that stress is anything that moves us from a state of balance (homeostasis) to imbalance (allostasis). Our body, naturally, through the autonomic nervous system (ANS) adapts to our environment, always seeking to bring us into balance. Humans have the unique ability to create stress inside the theater of the mind, however, the body doesn't know the difference, which leads to the body being in a constant state of alertness. This is cumulative and destructive, leading to massive interference in the short term and deadly health consequences in the long run.

Motivation

In Chapter 4 the concept of intrinsic motivation was explored. You know you have it when deep in your gut you really want something to happen; you have an inner drive, an unbounding level of energy to lean in and attack the process of successfully achieving a goal. The first phase of the flow cycle—struggle— again demands you find the right balance between your skills and how challenging a task or goal is. If you struggle with a clear sense of why you're attempting to do something—if your why is only moderately resonating with you as you take on the task—it will prevent you from getting in the zone. Why? You will not persevere through the struggle phase until you have a breakthrough and enter flow. The price of flow is suffering, and only those willing to go through the pain are able to access the profound levels of gain through flow.

Distraction

The management consultancy, McKinsey & Co., conducted a study on the work activities of white-collar knowledge workers revealing that on average, 60% of their time is spent on digital technologies and communication. This, by nature, leads to multi-tasking and shallow, low-value work. If flow follows focus, then digital distraction, and distraction of any kind, is going to prevent you from entering the zone.

Open office plans, while aimed at promoting collaboration, is a killer of flow. Interruptions by others prevent sustained, deep concentration on a task. In a training program I recently completed from the Flow Research Collective, statistics were cited relevant to levels of distraction an American worker experiences. They found that 70% are chronically distracted, only 2.3 hours of actual work is getting done, workers experience 56 interruptions per day, 44% of distraction is self-inflicted, and here is the stunner: Workers report only 11 minutes per day of complete focus.

Cal Newport, in his book *Deep Work,* calls this "shallow work," which he defines as non-cognitively demanding, logistical-style tasks often performed while distracted. He goes on to explain that these efforts, born out of multi-tasking, tend to inhibit the creation of new value in the world and are easy to replicate. A constant state of fragmented attention cannot accommodate getting in the zone, and worse yet, it becomes habit and makes getting into a focused state extremely difficult. If you want to achieve flow, then smartphones, your colleagues, and any kind of device must all be ruthlessly dealt with by intentionally engineering distraction out of your work setting so that you can create space and time to get in the zone.

Life Design

It's simple: If your day has no intentionality then whatever makes the most noise is going to get your attention. Poor life design, including an absence of goals, purpose, and structuring your day to optimize your energy and attention, will lead to massive interference. This interference works against your ability to get in the zone. Re-engineering your life is the biggest area of work when beginning your journey to a high-flow lifestyle to transform your performance and achieve your goals.

As I have stated repeatedly, developing a high-flow lifestyle is real work. Overcoming flow blockers is a process, not a one-time event. It will take time to become aware of your personal blockers and more time to work on them to the point where they are no longer a factor in your ability to achieve flow. This is a process of eliminating your interferences one at a time. In my own experience, it's been a journey. I believe creating a high-flow lifestyle is worth the effort because the payoff is enormous in both monetary success and richness of life. The pursuit of flow and simultaneous war on interference are lifelong pursuits.

Now that we have gone through the negative side of creating flow, it's time to transition to the positive side to talk about what catalyzes getting in the zone.

Flow Triggers

A vital truth to understand about flow is that it's trainable. You can learn to achieve flow at will, which is encouraging and motivating. I was a distracted, stressed, and burned-out entrepreneur with more flow blockers activated in my life than I can count, yet I was able to learn the fundamentals of flow and over time change my mindset and habits, gain knowledge, and re-engineer my life. You can do the same thing.

Flow has triggers that catalyze getting in the zone. The idea is to design into your life with as many of these triggers as possible until they're automatic. In this discussion of what catalyzes flow, you should begin connecting the dots between the information stated earlier in the book on managing stress, HRV, health habits, and psychology/mindset fundamentals because they all play a major role in creating the conditions to activate flow triggers. I will present individual flow triggers in this chapter, and in Chapter 12 team flow is discussed along with group flow triggers.

The main idea of flow triggers is that they drive attention into the present moment. Some triggers even cause dopamine and norepinephrine to increase, which drive focus and attention, while others reduce cognitive load. Cognitive load is the stuff that you're thinking about that add additional burdens to your working memory.

Curiosity, Passion, Purpose

If flow follows focus, then interest and curiosity naturally will trigger flow. When my son was growing up and struggling with ADD, he could name over 200 major league baseball players, he knew interesting facts about the teams, and he could demonstrate the batting stance of numerous star players, but he couldn't remember or focus on anything else. What he was interested in he could get lost in; without interest he would struggle. My son's story illustrates that having an interest in a goal or hobby is critical to experiencing the transformational effects of flow.

When I left my corporate banking career in the mid-1990s to start a business, I had passion, purpose, and a huge curiosity for it. Looking back, I was in the zone a lot and the sheer volume of work I was able to do then was amazing. The root was a white-hot passion and interest in being a successful business owner, which fed my energy, reading habits, and focus.

Clear Goals

If you have chosen a path that interests you and that you have a lot of passion for, it will be marginalized if you don't direct it toward the achievement of your goals. An airplane loaded with passengers leaves the terminal with a flight plan. If it didn't and simply took off and flew, eventually it would run out of fuel and crash. This analogy demonstrates the results one will experience when there's passion and interest but with no destination or plan—eventually he or she will run out of fuel and quit.

From the research by Locke and Latham, it's empirically proven that those with goals get better results than those without goals. You're reading a performance book, so you're undoubtedly looking for greater performance. Strong goals must be in your arsenal. Later in the book, a system of goal setting will be shared to empower you to use goals to accelerate your results.

Clear goals are a subset of goal setting. If you set a high-hard goal of closing $1 million of new business in a year, clear goals consist of the micro-goals that you set each day to build up to achieving your highest goal. For example, you would have to create a daily goal for specific prospects that you would call on, including contact information. By setting smaller, immediate goals, it enables you to focus on the task faster. A person lacking clarity in the moment of what to do will not get in the zone, instead becoming frustrated and likely digress to distractions to relieve the stress.

Challenge/Skill Ratio

In the next chapter you will learn about the flow cycle, where the first state is the struggle phase. The ratio of the challenge at hand to your skill level is a crucial concept you must grasp in order to learn how to achieve flow. If you have a growth mindset, you will accept challenges. As you struggle through challenge, you gain mastery. This is a virtuous cycle of learning new things, struggling to integrate that learning, practice, and growing a skill.

If you are at a point where the challenge is far greater than your skill, you will become anxious. If the challenge is too easy, boredom sets in. When you're in a game situation or starting a work task and the skill you bring is in close proximity to the level of challenge, this can catalyze a period of flow. Skill and knowledge are prerequisites of flow. I can get into flow by running, sitting at a café reading, writing, teaching, solving a business problem, or leading a team. At this point in my life, anything else you can imagine me doing would be a major struggle for me to get into flow. I believe I could learn something new and eventually achieve a flow state, however, today I don't have the skill to do so. As you can see, flow triggers build upon one another. Curiosity and passion drive a person through the challenge/skill ratio until they have developed the expertise to achieve the ratio of balance that allows them to get in the zone.

Complete Concentration

Focusing on the task at hand without interruptions or distractions is a major flow trigger. Focus cannot be achieved if you don't have the passion and curiosity along with the expertise. This is an engineering puzzle for you to solve and a habit to train. To attain complete concentration, your schedule and work environment must be designed for focus. You will need to restrict others' access to you for a defined period of time to allow yourself to focus on one thing. Remove anything from your workspace that can distract you from the one thing that you want to invest time in. Don't get discouraged; focusing your attention on one thing for any length of time takes practice. If you're like most people, you have succumbed to smartphone addiction at some level and have learned to check your phone dozens of times an hour. Think about any habits you have that could change to facilitate focus, then practice! The longer you focus, the more and the better you will be able to focus in the future.

Autonomy

The ability to spend time and energy on what you want to do, rather than a task handed to you by someone you report to or that's forced upon you by circumstances, will trigger flow. It stands to reason that if you have the autonomy to choose, you will choose that which is interesting and enjoyable to you. You will have to complete things like expense reports that you hate to do, however, when you're empowered with a choice, getting in the zone is likely, provided you have the habits and environment to capitalize on the opportunity.

Immediate Feedback

Flow is an enjoyable experience that provides incentives for developing skills and personal growth. Flow motivates you to pursue challenging activities, and in order to maintain flow, you have to set higher standards as skills progress. Flow enables you to live up to your individual potential. When you actively search for challenging situations that stretch your skills, you will develop even more skills. Immediate feedback is a necessary aspect of this process. To improve your skills, you need feedback on the level of your skills as often as possible in order to make adjustments until your skills improves. Feedback comes in the form of a partner with clear goals; clear goals tell you what you're doing and immediate feedback tells you how to do it better. If you know how to improve performance in real time, the mind doesn't wander off in search of clues for betterment.

Novelty

Novelty means surrounding yourself with a rich environment that involves finding things that will catch and keep your attention. I live close to Lake Michigan and I can visit a very nice park nearby that has

80+ acres of unspoiled hiking trails along the lakeshore. The views are breathtaking, which provides rich novelty and acts as a pattern interrupt to whatever I was fixating on prior to getting into that environment. Anything in nature will provide novelty.

I have spoken to many other entrepreneurs about this and I hear them universally say that when they go on vacation, their creative juices fire up. I've experienced this nearly every time I've taken time off and traveled to a new environment—my interest in reading increases, my pattern recognition kicks in, and new insights flow. To avoid annoying my wife, I've developed a habit of getting up very early on vacation so I can get in three hours of alone time to read, think, and enjoy some good espresso in a cool place. These moments are amazing, and they can induce flow.

Risk

If you want to get in the zone, take risk. For a basketball player that means being willing to take the three-point shot at a crucial moment deep in the game in front of 15,000 fans. For an entrepreneur, it's signing that deal or making that big decision. I can recall in April 1996 I was driving from Michigan to Milwaukee, Wisconsin with my wife to sign our first commercial lease. As the soon as the ink was dry, there was no turning back—we were on the hook for hundreds of thousands of dollars. Risk doesn't always mean financial or physical danger; it can also be an emotional, mental, and social risk. Either way, you must be willing to take risks. It's a sense of adventure and potential for failure that will concentrate your mind and drive you forward.

Complexity

Complexity simply means increasing the depth and breadth of your knowledge by seeking out information from many different sources or viewpoints. Warren Buffet's infamous partner, Charles Munger, is a proponent of multi-disciplinary reading—reading across a broad cross-section of subjects such as business, engineering, biology, and psychology. It trains the mind to think and to provide multiple models for evaluating investments and decision-making. The same applies to flow. It feeds your learning skills, which enable you to continue to navigate the challenge-and-skills relationship, growing personally as a way of life. Complexity will also feed pattern recognition, which leads to innovative insights, and complexity by nature forces you to concentrate to gain understanding. This trains your ability to focus attention, which drives flow.

Pattern Recognition and Creativity

Placing yourself in a creative situation can catalyze flow. In my research, I learned of a strategy author Steven Kotler has employed to accelerate pattern recognition, or making connections between multiple data points. Kotler will read 25 pages a day of fiction outside of his expertise and work focus to fire up his creative thought and pattern recognition.

Unpredictability

Unpredictability means being able to step outside your comfort zone and face the unknown. As you do this, the rush of doing so concentrates your mind on the task at hand, triggering flow. My friend Ron Wolforth, along with his wife Jill, owns the Texas Baseball Ranch. Ron has a great quote that I've used many times to encourage people to get out of their comfort zones. He says to the young pitchers he trains, "You must become comfortable being uncomfortable." So build unpredictability into your life and experience more time in flow.

Deep Embodiment

Deep embodiment means total physical awareness. When you can harness the power of your entire body paying attention to the task at hand, you will feel better and get in the zone more often. As you approach your focus time, use your five senses to perceive how you feel. Notice if your heart is racing or if you're relaxed. Often, I will do five minutes of deep diaphragmatic breathing prior to starting my focused work and it balances me, allowing me to become completely absorbed in the task at hand. Take notice if anything is off and work on it, or it will distract you and prevent flow.

At this point I hope you can appreciate that flow is a real event. The first time I learned these triggers I felt overwhelmed thinking I will never be able to incorporate all of them into my life. It's an investment of time and money to learn how to gain enough mastery of the science to see results in your work, sport, and personal life. But it's worth the investment.

If you're serious about achieving your goals, Tiger Performance Institute offers a path to mastering flow that's broken down into three smaller time and money commitments. It's further broken down into weekly lessons that enable you to learn and implement at a pace that is practical, given the realities of life. The richness of life and the joy of achieving at a level you never dreamed was possible is worth the struggle.

Now, we will get ready to learn about the flow cycle. You must learn to respect it, or you will not flow.

Implementation Checklist

✓ Assess the flow blockers in this chapter and which ones keep you from performing at your best.

✓ Assess the flow triggers. Which triggers could you begin to deploy today?

✓ Go to **www.tigerpi.com/online-courses/** and select the course that is best for based on your starting point with peak performance.

✓ Go to **www.tigerpi.com** and request a free consult if you want to learn more before making a course selection.

Chapter 7:

The Cycle of Flow

*"You can actually learn to turn on a natural inner switch to
sever those past mental patterns and activate breakouts that will
transform your daily life."*

— DR. HERBERT BENSON, MD,
Harvard

Understanding that flow is a cycle is paramount to actually experiencing flow. Why? Because knowing the cycle enables you to know where you are, what to expect, and where to go next as it relates to flow. Knowing the process will make getting through the struggle phase easier and will also create a burnout-proof path for the type-A personalities that always want more. Learning how the flow cycle can be integrated into your typical day and its activities can also be a game changer.

There are four stages to the flow cycle, each with a unique neurobiological and experience signature: Struggle, release, flow, and recovery. To achieve flow, you must work through each of the four stages. Without struggle, expertise never develops. Without experiencing the release or pattern interrupt stage, you can be stuck in the struggle phase and not get into the zone. When you struggle, work to change your thought patterns or activity, and move into the release, then flow is a time when amazing work or fun activities take place. However, flow is neurobiologically expensive. It's a time when five or six neurochemicals are firing all at once, which is the only time this happens. This means that when you come out of a period of being in the zone, recovery is a must, and this is where type-A personalities struggle. They believe recovery is a waste of time because they could be getting more done, and nothing could be further from the truth. Recovery rests the body and brain for future flow and the ability to work through the cycle again. No recovery means no flow. The flow cycle is to be respected and it's vital to understand that no one can live in flow all of the time.

My son Collin is left-handed, which is a massive advantage if you're a baseball pitcher. From the time he was nine years old, he was a pitcher. By age 12 we could see that he had real potential because he had unusually long arms and according to his coach at the time, something called a "fast arm." Thanks to this, we signed him up for individual lessons with a local Hall of Fame coach who was very good at developing young pitchers. For the next three years it was all struggle for Collin. He was working to unlearn bad habits, developing new mechanics, and having to apply it all in a game situation. Slowly he improved through junior high, JV, and then varsity baseball as a sophomore. He even had the opportunity to pitch for the varsity team as a freshman on one occasion. As he continued to work, his results improved.

During a district championship game, when playing for his mentor coach, Collin got in the zone. He entered the game in the third inning (he was a starting pitcher, but the team needed to change pitchers, so Collin was called in the moment), with his team down by one run. Fortunately, a teammate hit a two-run home run to put their Mona Shores Sailors team ahead 4-3 in the fourth inning. From the time Collin entered the game in this pressure-packed moment, he pitched shut-out baseball. His rhythm, command, and pace seemed to just flow each inning as the game progressed to its conclusion. In the seventh inning, with his team up by just one run, Collin got the first batter out. The second batter got on base by a walk, and in a great moment that I won't forget, Collin made an amazing move to first base, picking off the runner. He and his coach had worked on that move during every lesson for six years and in the moment when it counted most, he executed it flawlessly. The next batter hit a weak ground ball and his team won the district title game. It was one of the most fun games to watch and it's a small example of working through the flow cycle to get in the zone and perform at a high level.

Stage One: Struggle

The struggle phase can also be considered the loading phase. What it looks like also changes over time as you develop mastery. Your cortisol and norepinephrine levels flow as your stress mounts. When you struggle, the prefrontal cortex is hyper-active—you're taking in a lot of information. This stage is characterized by learning, training, and practice.

When I was beginning the process of writing this book, I was overwhelmed with the amount of information I had to research and synthesize into a manageable amount to organize into a book outline. Frustration and exhaustion reign in this stage because you're taxing your body and working memory. During this stage, you can't take your mind off the problem. Struggle can go on for hours, days, weeks, months, or even years. You can have multiple areas where you are struggling at once, too—at work on a project, with your overall work career, or with a hobby, such as golf. In a sense, you can have multiple flow cycles playing out at the same time in different domains. For instance, I have a cycle with this book. It's a cycle playing out the development of my company and finally, a cycle for my running hobby. I'm training to be a half-marathon runner and if you recall, I was a speed guy before, so running more than 400 meters is a novel activity for me.

Successfully moving through the struggle phase requires you to first maintain perspective. Remember: You are exactly where you're supposed to be. People with fixed mindsets fail here because they frame struggle as bad, but it's not! It's all part of the process. In a 2012 paper "The Flow Model Revisited," Johannes Keller, and Anne Landhäußer assert that the emergence of flow is basically dependent on a perceived fit of skills and task demands. This means that obtaining a flow state requires you to persevere (show grit) to develop until you've mastered the skills necessary for the challenge, and that the challenge/skill ratio is in balance or near balance. When you fight through the struggle phase, then you're ready for a breakthrough. As it says in the Bible, "Let perseverance finish its work so that you may be mature and complete."

Stage Two: Release

In this stage, the flow triggers that you employ enable you to release your mind from the hard-work mode and struggle. It's at this point, through a trigger activity that you let go and back off from the strain and struggle. The most important aspect of the release stage is that you must completely break away from prior thought and emotional patterns. During the struggle phase, you couldn't take your mind off the training, problem, or project, but in the release stage, you've got to let it go. In Chapter 6, major categories of flow triggers were explained; in reality, literally anything you do to interrupt your thinking pattern that changes your emotional state to rest can trigger flow. Going to an art museum, listening to music, doing the dishes, walking in nature—all of this can move you from struggle to release and usher you into flow.

Remember professor McEwen in Chapter 1 explained that there are three kinds of stress? There's good stress, tolerable stress, and toxic stress. Good stress is when you have a job interview, a speech, or a performance and your body adapts to meet the challenge, and when the challenge is over, you return to homeostasis. Think of the struggle phase as good stress and the release phase is you breaking out of stress mode into a balanced state again. If you stay in the struggle phase for too long, your fight or flight hormones will drag you down into mediocre performance. For type-A people, this is why building release triggers into your day are so important and recovery is necessary because you're setting the stage for super production.

As you engage in your flow trigger activity and change your thought patterns, your stress hormones are flushed away and feel-good neurochemistry is ushered into your brain. According to the research of Dr. Herb Benson, MD at Harvard University, the release stage involves the release, or puffs, of nitric oxide (NO) throughout the body, including in the brain. In turn, NO counters the negative effects of the stress hormone norepinephrine. As NO levels build, calming neurotransmitters, such as dopamine and endorphins, are released. As a result, blood vessels open, the heart rate decreases, the stress response fades, and inner tranquility takes over.

Dr. Benson's research has also found there are many other beneficial biochemical agents that activate in the release phase, including mood-enhancing, antibacterial, and immunity-bolstering molecules. When you trigger flow through the release stage, the release of NO and other beneficial biochemical agents provide you with an incredibly wide range of physical and psychological benefits. These include greater protection from disease, increased sense of well-being, and faster, more complete recovery from stress-related physical and emotional complaints. Finally, these benefits not only begin when you move into the release phase, they also continue throughout the entire flow cycle.

What is so exciting about getting in the zone when you respect the cycle is that you not only achieve great performance, but you also improve your mental and physical well-being. While you're achieving your goals, growing in mastery, and experiencing incredible growth overall, you're sowing the seeds of better health. Hopefully by now I've made my case on pursuing a high-flow lifestyle!

Stage Three: Flow

As a result of the many beneficial biochemical changes that took place through the release stage of the flow cycle, your mind and body is now ready for you to enter flow, or as Dr. Benson describes it, peak experience. Others describe flow as an optimal state of consciousness. In this stage of the flow cycle, where you're actually in flow, creativity is enhanced, learning accelerates, and productivity soars. We also feel our best and perform our best.

Steven Kotler describes what it looks and feels like to be in the zone better than anyone. He says,

"In flow, concentration becomes so laser-focused that everything else falls away. Action and awareness merge. Our sense of self and sense of self-consciousness completely disappear. Time dilates—meaning it slows down (like the freeze frame of a car crash) or speeds up (and five hours pass by in five minutes). And throughout, all aspects of performance are incredibly heightened—and that includes creative performance."

Kotler developed this acronym to describe the flow stage of the flow cycle is STER:

S – Selflessness - the inner critic goes quiet

T – Timelessness - time slows, freeze frame effect

E – Effortlessness - challenge and skill is in balance, work or action flows easily

R – Richness - great ideas, pattern recognition, and linking of ideas, all kick into high gear

This is the stage where your growth mindset, belief, and hard work to manage and improve your physiology pay off. You've invested in the practice for sport or hobbies and you've developed expertise over time, and through that practice and struggle, you are finally able to break into flow after you changed your pattern mentally and emotionally.

Getting in the zone and successfully cycling through each stage leads to better results and a long-term trajectory of growth. A sequence of events unfolds each time you work through the flow cycle. First you struggle with information loading and learning, then you build in pattern interrupting activities through triggers that usher in release, and finally you enter the zone where you gain new insights and produce at a very high level. As you work through this flow cycle and repeat it, your new normal elevates to a higher level of expertise, skill, and performance, which is a pattern that promotes better health and well-being alongside growing performance and expertise. The figure below illustrates the idea of applying grit to struggle, then getting in the zone and creating a virtuous cycle of growth.

There is, however, a downside to flow: You can become a bliss junkie, addicted to seeking the flow state and want to live there, disrespecting the cycle. It's a trap that will lock anyone who goes down this path out of flow. Peak performance is about consistency and pacing, not riding highs too high or lows too low. We want to avoid ending up depleted, so respecting the cycle is vital. The idea is to sustain elite performance over the long run. Bill Gates says, "Most people overestimate what they can do in one year and underestimate what they can do in ten years." Therefore, after the flow state has ended, we need to recover.

Stage Four: Recovery

Peak performers hate to shut down—just one more item on the to-do list or goal sheet today can be done if I go just a little longer! I was Exhibit A of this in the past. I drove my body and mind to produce non-stop, never wanting to take any time for recovery. Frankly, I didn't understand the need to recover at all. I thought sleeping was recovery and that I could cheat sleep as well and get more hours in to stay on task. This went on for 30 years, finally causing me to experience burnout. It's counterintuitive, but cycling recovery throughout your day, week, and on a quarterly basis, leads to higher productivity and insights than a straight-line of effort. In other words, less is more. As a type-A personality I would hate that phrase as some pithy saying by someone who only manifests results. I would mock them and say to myself, "While you're on the floor manifesting, I'm on the street producing."

The lesson here is to take timeouts during your day, each week for a whole day, and several days per quarter. Here are some suggestions for recovery:

- Build mini recovery breaks into your daily schedule through mindfulness, breath work, walks, etc.
- Get 8 hours of sleep each night, every night
- Drink the recommended water each day, consistently
- Do some form of movement every day—yoga, Tai Chi, walking, light exercise, stretching, etc.
- Get outside! Anywhere in nature will do; just take in the beauty
- Visualize and review what you did in flow and appreciate it with gratitude

The idea is to be gently active in recovery, not just sitting on the couch binge-watching TV all day. After a hard push in flow, move and relax and restore. Change your perspective, see recovery as building your reserves for the next upward cycle in flow where you gain new insights and advance your work to the next level. Recovery is a grit skill; develop the tenacity to recover, rather than grind on. When you grind on, the gears of your machine slow down and you end up being less productive than if you would've recovered in the first place.

The flow cycle is to be respected and understood. Once you understand the component parts, you can better design your life to get more flow. This takes time and is an iterative process where you experiment, evaluate, and repeat what works and discard what doesn't. While broad principles guide you in the process of achieving flow, how you get there is highly personal.

Something I learned is that you can have multiple flow cycles going on simultaneously. For example, writing this book became a daily micro-cycle. I went through a major struggle early on as I outlined the book contents, developed the research plan, and struggled through reviewing hundreds of research papers. As I began to fill in the research by chapter and summarize the articles, I could see chapters coming to life. All during this struggle phase I was also investing time in working out, going on nature walks, completing breathing exercises

THE CYCLE OF FLOW

between 90-120 work sprints, and just plugging away. When I began to write I got into the zone daily. The investment in the struggle phase and cycling my effort between work and recovery paid off. My daily two-hour time block for writing was super productive, enabling me to write the entire book in about eight weeks.

Simultaneously, I was learning to get in the zone as a runner, which has become one of my primary flow activities. The rhythmic and repetitive nature of a long run is conducive to getting into flow. Over the course of four months I extended my runs from three miles to half-marathon distance or 13.1 miles every two to three weeks as part of a training cycle. These longer runs were teaching me flow and as I have said a few times, the more flow you get, the more flow you get.

Finally, as I develop the company I started, I've realized that it represents a larger, longer-term flow cycle. The team and I labor through the struggle of testing processes, products, marketing approaches, all part of the struggle phase. We all understand that this is a longer-term cycle where the goal is to develop expertise in the struggle phase and compound that learning into improved product offerings and client experiences. As we do those things and respect the idea of oscillating our effort each day and with the use of project sprints in two-week cycles, we should see increasing periods of team flow. As team flow builds, growth will accelerate and our results will explode.

The figure below gives you a visual depiction of the flow cycle. It outlines the neurobiological signature of flow, showing the various neurotransmitters and hormones at work as you move through the flow cycle. It also explains the brain wave frequencies that are most pronounced during each stage of the flow cycle. Chief Neuroscientist at Tiger Performance Institute , Dr. Michael Mannino, PhD from the University of Miami, stresses with our team that the most important aspect of the flow cycle is simply understanding the stages, respecting them by applying a growth mindset, demonstrating grit through the struggle phase, applying flow triggers to get the release from struggle, and then once flow is over, investing in recovery. The actual brain waves at play and the neurochemicals flowing through your body at the time are less important, in terms of practical application. I share that information to undergird your belief in flow as a real event and not discard it as a mystical, anecdotal fad. Getting into the zone is a real phenomenon with serious implications for your future if you choose to pursue peak performance.

At this point in the book, you understand what getting in the zone is, the history of the research, and that you can trust the idea of flow being something real that you can pursue on solid ground. You also understand that it's necessary to respect the flow cycle, have learned to repeat it, and most importantly, how to recover properly for the next one. To take the next step, to begin to experience flow and repeat it, you must learn how to engineer your life for flow. In the next three chapters you will learn that the fundamentals, if mastered, will lead to more flow in your life.

Implementation Checklist

- ✓ What are your core areas of expertise, developed over several years?
- ✓ Do you have hobbies you have developed expertise in? Carve more time out for them to get into flow in your hobbies.
- ✓ If you have no expertise with hobbies, begin a new hobby and apply a growth mindset and grit toward the new hobby to get into flow.
- ✓ Build short recovery breaks into your typical workday.

Chapter 8:

Freeing Your Brain for Flow

"What is essential; to do less better."
—Marcus Aurelius,
Roman Emperor

Leverage

You're always going to be limited on the amount of time available each day to sleep, handle your personal hygiene, eat, pursue your goals, and be with your family. Your time is a fixed constraint. Time is input- and activity-focused, not output- and accomplishment-focused. If you measure your progress in terms of time, you'll forever remain a slave to your creation. If you measure your progress in terms of hours worked, you optimize the wrong thing. A time orientation leads to an increase in inputs, not output. Focusing on time you put in promotes a philosophy of do more, not produce more. This deleverages you, producing the opposite result. You must reimagine productivity by disconnecting our association between time and productivity. Leverage then must become the focal point. Time is fixed while leverage, in a sense, is infinite. Leverage is an amazing tool to deploy; a fixation on time will only lead you to run faster, while leverage enables you to run smarter.

Flow is a form of leverage. It expands what you can do in an hour, allowing you to do more with less. It enables you to untether from the chains of a "time equals output" mindset. It also catalyzes a virtuous cycle of introducing leverage, reducing time spent on a task, increasing output per unit of time, and encouraging you repeat the process as you find more opportunities for leverage. By learning to restructure how you work, you can train your attention on one thing, which is critical to achieving your goals, and repeat this process over and over. If the research is valid—which it is—and you can get 500% more accomplished while in flow, then this is incredible leverage that you can apply to the most important goals you have.

Leverage enables you to do your best so you can work your best in flow, fully absorbed in high-value, deep work. Examples of leverage include a real or virtual assistant, automating repetitive tasks, utilizing a vendor for a total outsource solution, and leveraging through people you add to the team. An example in business is Michael Kulp, CEO of a large chain of KFC and Taco Bell franchises. Kulp started with one location and pursued a vision to grow a chain of restaurants. Kulp has over 500 locations, which provides him massive leverage through people and systems to focus only on what he does best. The takeaway is to hunt for leverage everywhere and constantly attempt to do more with less. Ask yourself this question: "What would I have to do to cut my work hours in half while increasing my output?" You won't necessarily do this, but the thinking will yield opportunities to enlist leverage to increase your output in the same amount of time. You might also consider working less!

Your Brain is a Horrible Filing Cabinet

One form of leverage is to reduce cognitive load. Cognitive load refers to the amount of occupied working memory resources. Cognitive load theory differentiates cognitive load into three types: intrinsic, extraneous, and germane. Intrinsic cognitive load is the effort associated with a specific topic; extraneous cognitive load refers to the way information or tasks are presented to a learner; and germane cognitive load refers to the work put into creating a permanent store of knowledge, or a schema.

Cognitive load theory was developed in the late 1980s from a study on problem solving by Australian psychologist John Sweller. Sweller argued that instructional design can be used to reduce cognitive load in learners. Much later, other researchers developed a way to measure perceived mental effort, which is indicative of cognitive load. Information may only be stored in the long-term memory after first being attended to and processed by the working memory. Working memory, however, is extremely limited in capacity and duration and these limitations can impede learning and performance. Heavy cognitive load can have negative effects on task completion, which relates directly to performance. The central idea of cognitive load theory, as it relates to performance, is that you must consider the role and limitations of your working memory when you design your workday to increase performance. With increased distractions, particularly from cell phone use, social media access, and open-office systems, you are more prone to experience a high cognitive load, which can reduce learning and task completion success. Heavy cognitive load is a form of interference and according to the performance formula (Performance = Skill - Interference), reduces performance. Cognitive load is an anti-pattern to achieving flow as well.

The elimination of multi-tasking and chunking of information and tasks into groups are proven ways to reduce cognitive load. Your working memory imposes severe limitations on the amount of information you're able to receive, process, and remember. Over his illustrious career, George Miller, professor at Harvard, MIT, and Princeton, published an article in 1956 titled "The Magical Number Seven Plus or Minus Two: Some Limits on Our Capacity for Processing Information." Miller's research revealed a magic number seven, which is the maximum number of items or ideas that you can hold in working memory at once. By organizing tasks or information simultaneously into a sequence of chunks, you can break (or at least stretch) this informational bottleneck.

Time Perception

Let's start this section with a truism called Parkinson's Law. This law was first articulated by Cyril Parkinson in 1955. He derived the dictum from his extensive experience in the British Civil Service. Parkinson's Law is the adage that "work expands so as to fill the time available for its completion." Other uses of the concept are that work complicates to fill the available time. The first referenced meaning of the law has dominated and sprouted several corollaries, the best known being the Stock-Sanford corollary to Parkinson's Law: "If you wait until the last minute, it only takes a minute to do." Other corollaries include Horstman's: "Work contracts to fit in the time we give it;" and Asimov's: "In ten hours a day you have time to fall twice as far behind your commitments as in five hours a day." Each of these corollaries to Parkinson's law illustrate the idea that your perception of time affects your output potential.

The first story to illustrate the idea of how you perceive time when completing a major task is of author Steve Kotler when he writes a book. At a conference I heard Kotler share a story that illustrates the main point of this section on time perception. It was 2007, and he was facing some financial pressures. Kotler couldn't write anything in May, June, or July and was up against a deadline shortly in September. Stressed out, he went downhill mountain biking (his flow trigger) and it kicked him into the zone. He started to write and over the course of a two-week period he was able to write 190 pages of his latest book.

You arbitrarily assign time estimates to a task that are basically assumptions that you can readily adjust by reframing our perception of how long it takes to do something. These mental blocks are real. The story of Roger Bannister illustrates this idea of breaking through time perceptions perfectly. In an excerpt from the *Harvard Business Review* article, "What Breaking the 4-Minute Mile Taught Us About the Limits of Conventional Thinking," (March 2018), author Bill Taylor writes,

> Most people know the basic story of Roger Bannister, who, on May 6, 1954, busted through the four-minute barrier with a time of three minutes, fifty-nine and four-tenths

of a second. But it was not until I decided to write about him for my book *Practically Radical*, that I understood the story behind the story—and the lessons it holds for leaders who want to bust through barriers in their fields. Bryant reminds us that runners had been chasing the goal seriously since at least 1886, and that the challenge involved the most brilliant coaches and gifted athletes in North America, Europe, and Australia. "For years milers had been striving against the clock, but the elusive four minutes had always beaten them," he notes. "It had become as much a psychological barrier as a physical one. And like an unconquerable mountain, the closer it was approached, the more daunting it seemed."

This was truly the Holy Grail of athletic achievement. It's fascinating to read about the pressure, the crowds, the media swirl as runners tried in vain to break the mark. Bryant also reminds the reader that Bannister was an outlier and iconoclast—a full-time student who had little use for coaches and devised his own system for preparing to race. The British press "constantly ran stories criticizing his 'lone wolf' approach," Bryant notes, and urged him to adopt a more conventional regimen of training and coaching.

So, the four-minute barrier stood for decades, and when it fell, the circumstances defied the confident predictions of the best minds in the sport. The experts believed they knew the precise conditions under which the mark would fall: It would have to be in perfect weather (68 degrees and no wind), on a particular kind of track (hard, dry clay), and in front of a huge, boisterous crowd urging the runner on. But Bannister did it on a cold day, on a wet track, at a small meet in Oxford, England, before a crowd of just a few thousand people.

When Bannister broke the mark, even his most ardent rivals breathed a sigh of relief—*At last, somebody did it!* And once they saw that it could be done, they did it too. Just 46 days after Bannister's feat, John Landy, an Australian runner, not only broke the barrier again, but with a time of 3 minutes 58 seconds. Then, just a year later, three runners broke the four-minute barrier in a single race. Over the last half century, more than a thousand runners have conquered a barrier that had once been considered hopelessly out of reach.

Your brain tells you stories, but a new record causes you to change that story and you can then start imagining the impossible. You have to see yourself doing the impossible or at least performing at a higher level. You have to believe it's possible to achieve something far greater than you're achieving today. Change the story inside your mind and change your perception of the time it will take to achieve it. Start today by looking at the most important tasks you have to do and reflect on your normal time assumptions to complete it. Then cut the time to do it down to one third the amount of time and go do it. It will amaze you what you can do in one third the time. You have to rid your perfectionist tendencies, remember good is good enough, and experience the fun of completing things in one-third the time. Ultimately, the amount of time you allocate to the completion of a task is the biggest determinant of how long it actually takes.

All of what you're reading is meant to be integrated with other strategies. As you slowly learn to integrate more and more of the flow habits and strategies, your ability to do more in less time will emerge stronger. As you incorporate more and more of what you are reading, consider implementing a 35-hour work week. Imagine the time you would get back to pursue hobbies, relationships, and health by not working 60 hours a week. Some will scoff at that idea, which is fine, but others won't and will create an incredible new life out of their willingness to risk and try something new.

Eradication

The word "eradication" is bold and strong and communicates pushing the envelope. It sounds radical and this is the mindset I want to encourage you to take on as you look at your day-to-day activities and what you allow on your calendar. The fundamentals of this chapter are about reducing cognitive load, or the demands you place on your working memory. If you can reduce cognitive load, it will lead to flow.

Holding a lot of information in working memory at any given time exerts a significant toll on you by using a certain amount of fixed cognitive capabilities you have for that day. Think of it like RAM (random-access memory) in your computer; if you leave too many programs open, it bogs down processing speed. It's the same thing with your brain—try to hold too many thoughts in your head at once, and its processing slows down.

Constraint is defined as a limitation or restriction. Time constraints make it impossible to do everything. The total space of all possibilities is limitless, so it's not possible to pursue multiple ideas because it's unworkable. Roman statesman and philosopher Cicero said, "To become completely free one must become a slave to a set of laws." Meaning that a decision, a rule, or a principle that you choose to live by removes freedom in one area or direction and enables you to experience greater freedom in the direction you want to move.

An example of a daily task requiring cognitive load that can be automated, optimized, or eliminated is deciding each morning what to wear. Some people wear the same thing every day to eliminate this decision. Others pick out their outfit the night before, which is optimizing the task, eliminating cognitive load in the morning.

To implement the concept of eradication to lower cognitive load and get into flow more, think about what your primary, high-value work areas are and then build a fortress around them. Eliminate as much as you can from your day outside your high-value activities, or at minimum optimize what you can't eliminate. In my business, I've identified five high-value areas: health, writing, learning, marketing, and sales. If a task doesn't fit into one of those areas, it gets eliminated, optimized in a repeatable system, or delegated. If I can't do any of those, then I have about an hour block of time each day for tasks that I don't enjoy for things like email, certain administrative duties, etc.

Simplification

The 14th-century English theologian and philosopher William of Occam is credited with Occam's Razor. Webster defines this rule as "a scientific and philosophical rule that entities should not be multiplied unnecessarily, which is interpreted as requiring that the simplest of competing theories be preferred to the more complex or that explanations of unknown phenomena be sought first in terms of known quantities." In other words, keep it simple. Simplicity is preferred over complexity. The 19th-century Scottish philosopher Sir William Hamilton linked Occam's Razor to the idea of cutting away extraneous material, giving us the modern name for the principle.

Most people evolve in their professional lives to have scattered resource allocation, or doing a little of a lot of things. Too many things lead to fragmented energy and focus and ultimately shallow work. Fragmented resource allocation adds to cognitive load and works against getting in the zone. British novelist and teacher, Amelia Barr said, "It is always the simple that produces the marvelous." You want to simplify your life so much that your time, energy, and attention are uber-focused in your high-value areas, the things you value the most. Peak performers have concentrated cognition; they're like a laser beam of focus. Laser beams can cut through objects, while disco balls, which represent scattered attention, only put pretty lights on the wall.

The best insights come from breaks as you learned in the chapter on the flow cycle. You need space and time to get to the release phase, and if you fill your life to capacity, the space for breakthroughs doesn't exist. You need to redefine life balance. Many people believe a little bit of everything is good. Learning to choose what you focus on inside your high-value areas is the next level of simplification that will enable you to concentrate only on the very best activities to propel you toward your goals.

How do you achieve optimal balance? By discerning what should be done simultaneously and what should be done later. I can give you an example from my business to make this point clearer. As I was writing this book, I was moving from pilot phase to full launch of Tiger Performance Institute . Making the choice to live out the principles in this book, I have limited my work hours to 35 hours per week. To do this, something had to give, because the workload involved with a start-up is enormous. I used this filter of simultaneous vs. later to prioritize my focus and it has worked incredibly well.

I had the option to write this book, develop a podcast, create an online course, develop the company website, and expand the market segments beyond peak performance for individuals to teams, university athletic departments, and clinical settings. I initially decided that for a 120-day period I would focus on three areas simultaneously because they reinforced or enhanced each other. I chose to write this book, create an online course, and develop the website (I concentrated on organization and copy). This enabled me to put total focus on those three items over four months and complete each much faster and with more quality. After this four-month focus period, I reassessed and shifted to the development of a monthly print newsletter, the development of a podcast, and marketing the peak performance education and coaching services, again, because doing these three in tandem enhanced each strategy. After the second group of priorities are complete, I will pivot and begin to further develop the team flow program for businesses and athletic programs. If I attempted to do all of this at the same time, my focus would be so fragmented that it would've been difficult to do any of it.

Your task now is to implement this strategy of simplification by developing your high-value, priority work areas as well as personal areas. Determine what can you eradicate from your life to reduce cognitive load, then simplify your life by rebalancing priorities by considering if you should do something in parallel or sequentially based on if they enhance or detract from your short-term goals.

Implementation Checklist

- ✓ Assess your cognitive load today. Are you taxing it heavily by keeping things in short-term memory?
- ✓ Where can you apply leverage to gain back more time?
- ✓ Take one project you are working on, cut by 2/3 the allotted time and then complete the project to demonstrate the power of time perception.

Chapter 9:

You, a Corporate Athlete?

"If executives are to perform at high levels over the long haul, they have to train in the same systematic, multi-level way that world-class athletes do."

— JIM LOEHR AND TONY SCHWARTZ,
authors of "The Making of a Corporate Athlete"
in the Harvard Business Review

High performers in every realm such as entrepreneurs, lawyers, accountants, investment bankers, consultants, and artists, live with the expectation that work will be a priority. The "always on" work ethic leaks out into all times of the day and most believe this mindset is essential if they and their firms are to succeed in the marketplace.

Some performers thrive under pressure while others slowly grind down to exhaustion or worse, burnout. Is this only a mental issue? It's not; sustained peak performance demands physical and emotional strength as well as excellent cognitive function. To bring mind, body, and spirit to peak condition, performers need to learn what world-class athletes already know: Recovering energy is as important as expending it. To get in the zone, managing your energy is as important as all other the tools mentioned in this book.

Harvard researchers Leslie Perlow and Jessica Porter examined the impact of making time off predictable and required in a difficult industry: Management consulting. Perlow and Porter conducted two studies—the first to enforce taking one day off in the middle of the week each week and the second to refrain from doing any work one evening per week after 6pm to recover.

The study was conducted at the renowned Boston Consulting Group over a four-year period in several of BCG's North American offices. Here is an excerpt from their research that was published in the *Harvard Business Review*:

> The concept was so foreign we had to practically force some professionals to take their time off, especially when it coincided with periods of peak work intensity. Their first experiment tested predictable time off at an extreme level because consultants were required to take off a full day, in the middle of the work week. As a partner put it, "Forcing a full day off was like tying your right hand behind your back to teach you to use your left hand. It really helped the team overcome the perception that they had to be on call 24/7."
>
> In our second experiment, we required each consultant to take one scheduled night off a week, during which he or she could not work after 6pm—not even check or respond to e- mails or other messages. Again, we met with resistance from the consultants, even though the time off in this experiment was outside the client's normal working hours. The general practice among consultants on the road is that they work very hard while away from home, but then they hope to have a reasonable day on Friday when they are back in the home office, and they want the weekends off. As a project manager summed up the skepticism surrounding the night-off experiment, "What good is a night off going to do? Won't it just force me to work more on weekends?"

In both experiments, Perlow and Porter reported that employees felt tension between their commitment to taking time off and what they felt they owed both the client and their teammates. Some consultants were concerned that taking the time off, while other peers were grinding away, would shed negative light on them. One consultant is quoted in Perlow's article saying, "If you are making promotion decisions, and you look at someone who has been staffed on a project where she is really cranking it out and working long hours, and you compare that to someone who is getting a day off, it is hard to believe you are not going to promote the person who appears to be working harder." This consultant was clearly linking hours worked to results rather than outcomes.

This kind of thinking reinforces a vicious cycle. Perlow and Porter said, "Responsiveness breeds the need for more responsiveness. When people are 'always on,' responsiveness becomes ingrained in the way they work, expected by clients and partners, and even institutionalized in performance metrics." The 24/7 cycle of an always-on work mindset can be broken if one understands the alternative and the obvious downsides to relentless work. Perlow and Porter proved in a difficult setting that productivity increases when you actually do less.

Burnout

In the introduction I made the case for why we need to accelerate learning and sustain elite performance. The meta trends driving this need are massive technological change and ever-increasing pressure to deliver results in a hyper-competitive world. Showing up and being steady are no longer enough. You must do deep work and deliver real value or risk losing out to technological change that's wiping away businesses and causes jobs to be repetitive or shallow in value by nature. Historically, performance has been judged by what goes on above the neck. My goal is to help you see the important link between the brain, the body, and the mindset collectively. If you fail to take time off and oscillate your energy expenditure, you will begin to slow down, your productivity will wane, and burnout will set in.

Burnout is a prolonged response to chronic emotional and interpersonal stressors on the job and is defined along three dimensions:

1. Overwhelming exhaustion
2. Cynicism and detachment
3. A sense of ineffectiveness and lack of accomplishment

Sustained elite performance is the result of a systems view. You have multiple major body systems such as the endocrine system, the cardiovascular system, and the nervous system, to name a few. Your mental health is a system as is your mindset. All of these systems interact with each other, and when you fail to take care of yourself in one area, it has a negative effect on all of the systems. Sustained or chronic imbalances in one or more of your systems leads to problems all over your body.

Burnout, like flow, is a state of consciousness, only on the negative side. Overwork and lack of recovery are contributing factors, but high job demands, low control, and effort-reward imbalance are risk factors as outlined by the World Health Organization (WHO). The WHO also classifies burnout as a diagnosable disorder. Burnout is death by 1,000 cuts—the accumulation of thousands of tiny disappointments that stack upon one another.

Burnout emerges when demands on your systems outstrip your ability to cope over the long term. It's toxic stress, as defined earlier by Dr. Bruce McEwen, characterized by feelings of emotional exhaustion, negatively directed at everyone. It includes a crisis in feelings of professional competence. Much like symptoms of depression, burnout will choke off your ambition, idealism, and sense of worth.

Research by the Karolinska Institute in Sweden and the Stress Research Institute at Stockholm University reveals that there is a neurophysiology of burnout that alters neural circuitry and leads to a downward spiral. Burnout enlarges the amygdala and fractures connectivity, weakening the connection to other brain regions. This leads to difficulty regulating emotions, leaving us feeling on edge and easily angered. Burnout leads to reduced cognitive function, lowering executive functioning, ultimately weakening impulse control. Working memory, problem solving, and creativity also all decline with burnout.

The good news is that you can reverse the effects of burnout. My own story is case in point. I experienced all the symptoms and outward consequences of burnout and have gone through the process outlined in this book to completely improve my health and overcome burnout. Tiger Performance Institute utilizes the Maslach Burnout Inventory assessment when working with someone who is suffering from burnout. The MBI is a globally recognized tool validated by 35 years of research and used in 88% of burnout research. Tiger Performance Institute can help you establish a baseline and then help you build new habits to overcome the performance destroying the effects of burnout.

Recovery: The Answer to Sustained Peak Performance

Getting in the zone, or achieving flow, is an optimal experience followed by a low. Recovery is crucial to preparing for the next phase of the flow cycle and to having any chance of sustaining high levels of performance. What does it look like to build recovery into your life? It's about becoming a non-professional, executive athlete. For any type of competitive athlete, time spent training makes up the majority of their "work" time. The time actually spent in competition is a small percentage of an athlete's overall time. However, non-professional, executive athletes are the opposite. Those who produce in the marketplace, in university labs, and on stage tend to invest a small amount of time on training and the majority of time competing. Most stay continually in stress, stretching energy expenditure for days, weeks, months, and years. That was my life. If you want to break this cycle, you need to make recovery a priority. It's not a time-out; it's part of your skill development, it's part of being productive.

An executive athlete must come to understand that their time during the day is fixed but the quantity and quality of energy available is variable. Energy is a lever of performance, just like time leverage. The key idea to becoming an executive athlete and building recovery into your life is the idea of oscillation.

Oscillation is the idea of alternating between the short-term stress of performing a task followed by a period of recovery. For example, in my day, I block out two hours first thing in the morning for my most important tasks. Then I go for a walk with my wife and our dog. Thirty minutes later, I'm refreshed mentally and physically for the next two-hour block. Other recovery options are breathing exercises, meditation, or a short nap—anything that's 15-30 minutes long. The key is the oscillation, not continuous performance. Live like a tiger who hunts then sleeps and repeats that cycle over and over. To perform optimally, we need to oscillate. Oscillate each day, and create a weekly, monthly, and quarterly pattern of oscillation. The graphic below visually depicts this cycle of performance and stress, followed by a period of recovery, enabling you to adapt and perform at an even higher level.

Adaptation

Stress + Recovery = Adaptation

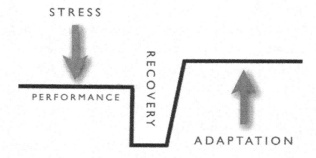

When you work continuously in a linear fashion, as most average performers who fail to oscillate do, you run into the law of diminishing returns on your time. If you continue to grind on, your expanding workload will cause performance to drop off as your energy and attention begins to wane.

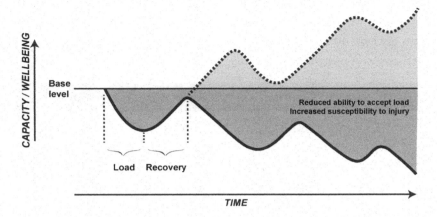

The rhythmic life of the executive athlete can be characterized as a series of micro-cycles within a day, week, month, and even a year. As you expend energy and attention and experience the stress of completing a task, you will begin to run up on the law of diminishing returns. At this point, you cycle down, recover, and then enter your next energy and attention expenditure. As you work through this on-and-off cycle, you should trend up in terms of performance. We see this same phenomenon with athletes using heart rate variability. If they cycle their training and recovery, HRV increases will reflect the discipline of oscillation. I have seen this personally as I train for running half marathons.

What are some good practices to ensure that you have good recovery protocols? The first two chapters give you a detailed guide, but the highlights are:

1) Know you need recovery
2) Practice good sleep habits
3) Hydrate
4) Engage in active recovery

Active recovery includes walking, light stretching, light yoga, hiking, getting out in nature, using the sauna, or getting a massage, to name a few activities.

In summary, build into your schedule on and off periods. It's counterintuitive and it's hard if you're type A, but a straight line of energy expenditure for 8-12 hours over an extended period of time is a prescription for burnout. So, become a corporate athlete, oscillate your energy expenditure, and watch your results grow. If high-priced consultants can learn how to do this, you can too.

Implementation Checklist

✓ Change your mindset on work. Think like an athlete by building time blocks for both performance and recovery.
✓ Begin taking nature walks a few days a week.
✓ Consider the Tiger Synchronize coaching program. Go to www.tigerpi.com/coaching-programs/

Chapter 10:

Little Distractions That Rob You Blind

"If you wanted to invent a device that could rewire our minds, if you wanted to create a society of people who were perpetually distracted, isolated, and overtired, if you wanted to weaken our memories and damage our capacity for focus and deep thought, if you wanted to reduce empathy, encourage self-absorption, and redraw the lines of social etiquette, you'd likely end up with a smartphone."

—CATHERINE PRICE,
author of How to Break Up with Your Phone:
The 30-Day Plan to Take Back Your Life

Minnesota Institute of Psychiatry researcher Dr. Aviel Goodman, in his literature review of the neurobiology of addiction, found that there is an underlying biopsychological process that addictive disorders share. The addictive process is an interplay of impaired operations of three functional systems: motivation-reward, emotional regulation, and behavioral inhibition (someone given to distress and nervousness in new situations). Dr. Goodman quotes in the study that:

> The addictive process can be defined as an enduring, inordinately strong tendency to engage in some form of pleasure-producing behavior in a pattern that is characterized by impaired control and continuation despite significant harmful consequences. The class of addictive

> disorders includes psychoactive substance addiction, bulimia, pathological gambling, shopping or buying addiction, sexual addiction, and other enduring conditions in which a behavior that can function both to produce pleasure and to reduce painful affects is employed in a pattern that is characterized by two key features: (1) recurrent failure to control the behavior, and (2) continuation of the behavior despite significant harmful consequences.

It's hard to read this quote by Goodman and not see the correlations or similarities to the daily battle most people wage with technology and social media. In Robin Sharm's book *The 5:00am Club*, he pounds away at the concept that our addiction to distraction is costing us our fortune. Technology at the consumer level is designed like an injection of an addictive drug; it activates the brain's reward pathway to increase usage. When reading Dr. Goodman's research, you can discern the parallels between substance abuse and tech addiction.

Another quote by Catherine Price puts this addiction to distraction in context:

> Every moment of attention we spend scrolling through social media is attention spent making money for someone else. The numbers are staggering: A *New York Times* analysis calculated that as of 2014, Facebook users were spending a collective 39,757 years' worth of attention on the site, every single day. It is attention that we did not spend on our families, or our friends, or ourselves. And just like time, once we have spent attention, we can never get it back. This is a really big deal because our attention is the most valuable thing we have. We experience only what we pay attention to. We remember only what we pay attention to. When we decide what to pay attention to in the moment, we are making a broader decision about how we want to spend our lives.

Whether it's your fortune, lost time on your goal, or lost time with those you love, distraction comes with a grave cost in the form of lost opportunities, time, and memories. The sad fact is that this level of distraction is the norm in our society. It's also your opportunity and differentiator if you can control your attention and focus because flow follows focus. Learning to manage your technology use and environment will lead to deeper, more thoughtful work that will translate into greater success.

Here are some statistics from the Flow Research Collective highlighting the state of distraction humans face. You experience 4.2 billion people, 1 billion websites, and 70 million advertisements all vying for your attention on a daily basis. You have to guard and police your attention or become a casualty to distraction. Always being on and having permanent availability and fragmented attention are the new norm. There's correlating evidence between media use and sleep deprivation. The speed of new technology is rapidly increasing. The time to grow to 50 million users went from 38 years for radio to one year for YouTube and 35 days for the game Angry Birds. This war on attention is making people unhappy, impairing cognition, and leading to people checking their phones 150 times a day. The addiction process seems to be at work with respect to technology and media and it messes with your motivation-reward center, impacts your emotional control, and can cause you to disengage from situations.

Dr. Ned Hollowell from Harvard University has gone as far as to define a new clinical attentional disorder: Attention Deficit Trait (ADT). A person with ADT is a mess. They tap their fingers or knee, their legs are moving all the time, and this person is manically multi-tasking: checking email, talking on the phone, checking other apps on their phone, etc. Colleagues cannot hold this person's attention for more than a minute or two. This person lives with inner frenzy, is impatient, and has difficulty organizing time and keeping appointments. ADT is on the rise, increasing by a factor of 10 over the past decade, and behavior, environment, and technology are the underlying causes. The major point to take away from this is that ADT, or anything remotely resembling it, is the enemy of flow. If you're honest with yourself, I'm sure you can think of moments or days where you resembled a person with ADT and it cost you dearly that entire day.

Dr. Adam Grazzaley, a professor at the University of California in San Francisco and author of the book, *The Distracted Mind: Ancient Brains in a High-Tech World*, explains in his book the daily struggle with distraction from this information-saturated world. He introduces the concept of interference to describe interruption and distraction. Goal interference is when you have decided to do something, focused your attention, and something takes place to hinder that goal. You have been built to be able to delay your response when you perceive an interruption through evaluation and decision making. You can engage, act, and call on working memory, attention, and goal management capabilities. These abilities enable you to operate in this dynamic world in a goal-oriented manner and deal with interference. As you face a distracting world, it's important to understand these abilities and their limitations. Dr. Grazzaley outlines strategies to reduce goal interference:

1) Reduce task switching
2) Know how you think
3) Put your smartphone out of sight when working or with people
4) Exercise regularly to enhance control of cognitive abilities
5) Utilize breathing techniques

A Commitment to Depth

The evidence is abundant: People are distracted, addicted to distractions, and the quality of work is suffering as the world is moving through the Great Restructuring. More than ever, you need to be focused and doing your best work, or you're going to be stuck at your worst. How do you overcome your overload perception and take back control of your life to do your best work? Let's first define overload and how people get overloaded before you can work on clearing it.

Overwhelm is the perception that the current demands you face exceed the resources you possess to meet them. Overwhelm is a form of cognitive load and plays a role in the challenge/skills balance, which is a prerequisite for getting in the zone. When the challenge is greater than the skill, it leads to anxiety and overwhelm. When skills significantly exceed the challenge, boredom ensues. Simplistically, you resolve being overwhelmed by increasing resources or lowering load.

Strategies to solve overwhelm include: A five-minute breathing exercise that engages the parasympathetic system; listing out all you have to do and chunking tasks into logical groups and reprioritizing completion deadlines; taking a few minutes to write out what you're grateful for; and taking 10-15 minutes during the day to do something you enjoy outside of work. These are baby steps and there are many more means to work through overwhelm. However, if you want to get in the zone, learning how to establish strategic goals and set up your day to avoid overwhelm is essential.

Clearing Your Life of Distraction and Training Your Attention

What is attention? At its essence, attention is the behavioral and cognitive process of selectively concentrating on a discrete aspect of information while ignoring all other perceivable information. William James, America's first psychologist, said, "attention is the taking possession by the mind, in clear and vivid form, of one out of what seem several simultaneously possible objects or trains of thought. Focalization and concentration of consciousness are of its essence." Pulitzer Prize-winning poet Mary Oliver said, "Attention is fundamental to all human experience. Art, science, connection to others, all begins with the ability to pay attention. To pay attention, this is our endless and proper work." Carefully directed focused attention is the source of all greatness.

The goal is maximizing the amount of time to be in flow where you will do your best work. Author Cal Newport formed something he calls the Deep Work Hypothesis. Deep work is the ability to concentrate attention to perform high-value work that the market values and it's becoming more valuable and rarer, and the few who cultivate this skill will thrive in this century of accelerating change. Before you can get in the zone, you have to clean out all distraction. There are two keys: 1) Eliminate all self-imposed distraction, and 2) protect your attention by eliminating all disruption that is externally imposed. Deal with what you do that leads you astray and change your environment so outside forces that distract you are minimized.

Here are practical steps you can take now:

- Stop multitasking, it doesn't work. You want depth, not shallow work.
- Avoid task switching. Be ferocious about doing one thing at a time.
- Constantly look for opportunities to reduce cognitive load.
- Make good sleep your number-one priority each night.
- Remove social apps from your phone.
- Turn off all notifications on your phone and computer.
- Close social apps in the browser if working on your computer with shared drives during your focus (flow) time.
- Reduce meetings as much as possible. I force most of mine to be on Mondays. Push for in-person, video chats, or phone calls and then compress further to email or text until you can get rid of unnecessary meetings altogether.
- Batch emails, phone calls, and texts to one time slot a day rather than constantly checking them, which is a form of task switching and adds cognitive load and leaves attention residue.
- Turn your phone off or place it in another room when in flow. Put the phone on "do not disturb" mode while in focus time.

Environmental Distraction Proofing

"What separates two people most profoundly is a different sense and degree of cleanliness."

–Friedrich Neitzche

The spaces you live and work in should reflect the person you are becoming now, not for the person you were in the past. Make your living and workspaces attractive and inspiring. An organized space:

1. Lowers anxiety to calibrate the challenge/skills balance
2. Lowers cognitive load
3. Facilitates clear goals
4. Reduces friction, hassle, stress, and agitation

Your Personal Environment Clean-up Action Plan:

1. Minimize variables—have the same desk, same setup, and keep it minimal
2. Eliminate sound disruptions—get noise-canceling headphones
3. Eliminate visual distractions—television screens, anything that causes you to look.
4. Maintain cleanliness—clutter creates negative emotion
5. Organize everything—what you need should be easily accessible without friction or cognitive overhead

Finally, take on the mindset that you cannot keep everyone happy. Allow some chaos to build up by not answering people who aren't demanding immediate responses. This will allow you to move from the trivial to the meaningful. People who are in chaos are always available, distracted, overwhelmed, live in struggle phase, and rarely ever get in the zone. People who do deep work, on the other hand, impact other people by their life's work. They measure success by output not time. They get in the zone often and they prize the meaningful and important over the trivial. Sure, some people will be annoyed, a small mess may build up, and a few smaller opportunities may be missed. But you must lose a little to gain a lot. Those who you fear will be amazed at what you accomplish and learn to live with the new you. Take a stand and annihilate distraction to get in the zone.

I leave you with this aspirational and inspirational quote that will attract the person who is committed to be the best they can be. It is up to you; you have a choice.

"Our work culture's shift toward the shallow is exposing a massive economic and personal opportunity for the few who recognize the potential of resisting this trend and prioritizing depth."

—CAL NEWPORT,
Author—Deep Work

Implementation Checklist

- ✓ Stop multitasking!
- ✓ Simplify and clean up your work environment.
- ✓ Break your addiction to tech, implement the suggestions in this chapter.

Chapter 11:

Now Multiply Your Greatness in The Zone

"Five small wins a day leads to 1,850 wins in 12 months. Consistency breeds mastery."

—ROBIN SHARMA,
author of The 5AM Club

Michel Lotito gained fame as a French entertainer known as Monsieur Mangetout ("Mr. Eat-All"). From an early age, he curiously would consume things no normal human being would consider. It all started with a broken drinking glass. Instead of sweeping up the mess, he cleaned up by eating the broken glass. What's remarkable is he suffered no negative side effects, but… Where were his parents?

Lotito later learned he had a condition known as pica, a psychological compulsion to eat non-nutritive objects. Typically, this is a health condition that creates health problems. However, Mr. Eat-All was able to chew the broken glass and swallow it, seemingly without any complications. Physicians examined Lotito and determined he had an extraordinarily resilient digestive system. His stomach and intestines were much thicker than average, allowing him to ingest things that would kill anyone else.

Lotito parlayed his unusual eating habits on the road as a performer, and people were eager to watch him eat the most amazing things. In the course of his career, Lotito consumed 18 bicycles, seven TV sets, two beds, 15 supermarket trolleys, a computer, a coffin (handles and all), a pair of skis and six chandeliers. All told, he ate over nine tons of metal.

The most impressive item Lotito consumed was an airplane. Yes, you read that correctly, an airplane. In 1978 he began munching on a Cessna 150 airplane. He ate it the way one is supposed to eat an elephant: one bite at a time. He meticulously broke down each part of the plane into small, finely-ground pieces that he could swallow and digest. It took him two years, but by the end of 1980, the entire airplane had disappeared into Lotito's stomach. Note the time element—he literally went through the daily grind (pun intended) for two years, breaking the airplane down into manageable pieces.

The Guinness Book of Records recognized Lotito for "The Strangest Diet." He was awarded a brass plaque for this honor—which he promptly consumed. Lotito died of natural causes shortly after his 57th birthday.

Lotito's successful consumption of an airplane is a fitting illustration of what it looks like to engineer an elite performance life. You choose a clear direction, you establish a path to pursue, you set goals, and then you execute your vision. You do this one task and one day at a time, akin to eating an airplane one bite at a time, and you compound this daily behavior into extraordinary results.

A Review of Your Foundation

At this point you know to layer on or stack intrinsic motivators such as vision, mission, purpose, and core values. You have a strong personal belief in your ability to achieve the goal. You own your results, good or bad, and you possess a growth mindset. You have the grit from past experiences and the personal alignment with your goals to achieve whatever you set out to do. Additionally, you initiated new habits like breathing to balance your autonomic nervous system and improve your health to give you all the energy you need to push out interference. You also understand what flow is, that you need to work through struggle as you gain expertise or skill, and the importance of a few primary flow activities outside of work to get out of the struggle phase and into release so you can flow. Finally, you understand that you must respect the flow cycle by building recovery into each day. Now you are ready to create a template for living to build automation into a daily routine.

A principle vital to learn and live for peak performance is cause and effect. An action today is a cause, the corresponding consequence of the action at some later time is the effect. The actions and behaviors exhibited daily will define your future, as consequences from prior actions and behaviors arrive at your door. Peak performance demands an acute awareness of the reality that day-to-day actions have consequences and must be scrutinized carefully. Elite performers understand the process and how it relates to cause and effect, while average performers want instant gratification. A lack of instant gratification is why people don't change; they fail to appreciate cause and effect and time lags involved to reach a pre-determined goal.

Author Darren Hardy explained in his book *The Compound Effect* that there is a two-year gap (see Fig. 1) between when the action or behavior change is initiated and the full effect or consequence of the change. People who grasp that there is a time lapse between a cause and the corresponding effect will embrace process and a long-game mentality. Today's actions don't show up immediately; we forget today's results are from our prior actions. Therefore, top performers invest time and energy in developing great daily habits, trusting the results will come when they formulate a plan and execute it daily.

Fig. 1

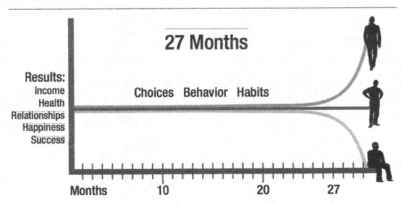

Building a Ladder to Elite Performance

To bring your vision alive and achieve your transformative purpose, intentional engineering is required. You would never get on a plane if you knew the crew had no flight plan, so similarly, you shouldn't pursue a vision without a clear plan built on goals. The best way to create a flight plan for your life is through a laddered goal system. Earlier in the book, validated research was shared establishing the fact that setting goals will enhance your motivation and performance. With this in mind, I will share a goal setting process that I've used for years, both personally and in organizational leadership roles, to drive goal achievement.

In his book *Execution: The Discipline of Getting Things Done*, Larry Bossidy wrote, "Execution is not just tactics—it is a discipline and a system. It has to be built into a company's strategy, its goals, and its culture." The quote relates to a corporate setting, but the parallel to personal goal setting applies. If you're seeking elite levels of performance, it requires a system, repeated daily over months and years to bring about the compound effect. Establishing a goal management system needs to become part of your personal culture.

The key to goal setting is alignment. We set goals based on our core values and in relation to our vision, mission, and transformative purpose. If you skip the hard work of gaining extreme clarity, your goal setting will be an exercise in futility. If you find your previous attempts at goal setting produced little fruit, it's because you failed to align those goals with your vision, mission, purpose, and values. When everything lines up, you gain the superpower of intrinsic motivation, which drives sustainable energy and grit toward a predetermined set of goals.

Goal-setting characteristics include specificity, measurability, difficulty, and relevancy. Recall the research by Latham and Locke supporting specificity and difficulty—the harder the goal, the better the performance, to a point. Also, the more specific the goal, the better the performance. Feedback is a key component of flow and understanding necessary changes that must be made to ultimately achieve a goal. If your goals are clearly measurable, they will provide the feedback you need to make course corrections. Finally, relevancy simply means they are in alignment with who you are desiring to become.

Goal Ladder

The concept of a goal ladder is nothing more than a cadence or rhythm of goal setting and review. However, despite its simple nature, execution is far from simple—it must build as a routine and be executed daily. To build your goal ladder, start with your big, transformative purpose—the thing you are willing to invest your life in. An example for a basketball coach could be to build into the lives of young men so that they become productive members of society and effective fathers in their homes. Once you establish that, you would work back from that big purpose, reviewing your vision and core values, to set long-term goals that serve your purpose and align with your vision and values. From there you continue to work backwards in terms of time all the way down to what you will do each day. This process of moving from 30,000 feet where vision resides to what you do tomorrow reduces cognitive load, gives you something to focus your attention on, and is in line with your purpose, ultimately fueling intrinsic motivation, passion, and energy. In other words, you are primed for flow every single day!

Transformative Purpose

Purpose is your why or your reason for being. It should be something that grips you to the core, that excites you, causing you to invest your life in the pursuit of this purpose. I encourage you to think big, expand your belief in what is possible, and visualize what your life would be like if you saw your purpose become reality. Notice the emotions and feelings that occur as you visualize your purpose being realized. This will take time; it's not a 30-minute exercise. It will take some seasoning in your subconscious to bring out the refined version of your true purpose. It's okay if you write it out and then change it several times; you have to refine it to what will motivate you to act. Purpose is the beginning of layering or stacking intrinsic motivators. The goal ladder represents a full stack of intrinsic motivation from the distant to the present moment, propelling you through days, weeks, months, quarters, and years of peak performance in pursuit of your dream.

Long-Term Big Goals

Gary Latham, father of goal-setting theory, studied goal setting and found that long-term, challenging goals give a 11% - 25% boost in motivation alone. This activates neurotransmitters in your brain to aid in motivation, getting your biology to work for you rather than against you. Long-term goals are typically 1-5 years in duration and represent a destination that you want to arrive at. They are the end-game outcomes that will result in your purpose being fulfilled. To use our basketball coach example, a junior varsity coach might set a long-term goal of becoming a varsity coach within the 1-5 years.

Annual Goals

When you look at annual goals, you begin to get into the repeating rhythm or cycle of setting priorities annually that then cascade down into daily tasks. The idea is to link what you do each day to an upward cascading set of goals and priorities that serve both your long-term goals and your vision, mission, purpose, and values. This is what it means to gain alignment, which when properly established, leads to massive intrinsic motivation. You become a force of nature with little outside support needed to generate the daily focused attention and energy to get into flow and make progress toward your goals.

Author John Maxwell has shared in several of his books and conferences the practice of taking a week each year to review the past year and review your mission, vision, and values. During this week you should set priorities for the following year. This is a critical step not to be taken lightly or attempted in a state of distraction. This exercise sets the course for the entire year so it's important to establish top goals for the next year and prioritize them by ranking them in a system such as A, B, or C. Review these goals often, visualize achieving them and how contribute progressively to the achievement of your long-term big goals.

Quarterly Goals

After establishing your annual goals, list out all of the steps needed to reach those goals. If your goal is to write a book, for example, you would develop the main idea, an outline or table of contents, list all of the research sources and publishers to approach, and schedule out blocks of time to write, then ultimately, complete the actual writing. After you have written out the steps to complete each of your annual goals, it's time to prioritize when you will complete each.

It's important to place these steps as goals you will pursue by quarter. You can't chase all of them at once—if everything is a priority, nothing is. Think in terms of the 80/20 principle, which states that a vital few of your actions will generate the majority of your results. The last step is to rank your goals in order for each quarter with a letter A for highest priority, B for the next level priority, and C for the lowest priority. While they are all valid goals and your vision includes completing all of them, however, some are more vital than others based on the value you've assigned to each goal. At this point, you're finished with planning the year and your work will transition to a more specific approach. At the beginning of each quarter, review your goals and decide if any adjustments are in order based on the changing realities of your industry and life.

Monthly Goals

As you arrive at the beginning of a new month, review your quarterly goals by priority and plan out the top goals for the month. A tool I like to use that I learned from Tony Robbins is what he calls the Massive Action Plan, or MAP. When I plan the next month, I first review how I've done that current month and then I note anything not completed, consider what I know needs to be done today, and I sit and make a list of all the tasks that I believe should be done in the next month. Again, this is based on my prioritized quarterly goals with a present focus on bringing the quarterly goals into the current month. I will use this monthly process to drive further into my weekly goals.

As mentioned earlier in Harvard Professor George Miller's classic 1956 article, "The Magic Number 7, Plus or Minus Two," he shared research on limits of our working memory. The paper suggests we should chunk information into groups to enable us to process information efficiently. The lesson here is to take your monthly goal plan and chunk it into groups of similar activities and use this list to establish your goals for the current month and in weekly planning. Remember, at each step, the goals or tasks should work to build up to the next level goal, ultimately toward the achievement of your long-terms goals, which serve your transformative purpose and are congruent with your core values.

Weekly Goals or Tasks

From your monthly goals and massive action plan, you now have the information to establish your weekly goals or tasks. You're essentially spreading your massive action plan over the four- or five-week period of each month. This is eating the airplane one difficult bite after another. In my organization, each person, including me, posts their goals for the week on Monday morning. We all post our monthly goals at the end of the prior month and repost our quarterly goals at the beginning of a quarter in our shared drive. Each person's goals are in alignment with their long-term goals, as well as their personal vision, mission, purpose, and core values. Additionally, each team member's goals are supportive of the organization's goals. We gain group flow from having this level of clarity built into our culture. I will delve more deeply into the notion of group flow in Chapter 12.

Recall that achieving flow follows focus. As you follow how this goal-setting system unfolds, you can observe how it's refining down at each level more specificity to necessary actions. Increasing clarity paves the way for increased attention on fewer, more vital activities that drive the accomplishment of goals.

Daily Scripts

The last step in the refining process is to develop a day script that works for you. A daily script is your road map for a specific day. You need a way to declare a day a win and your script provides you the feedback to understand if you won or lost that day. The idea is to repeat the completion of successful days over and over and get the power of compounding working for you. Again, to be a peak performer, it's vital that you have a way to declare your day a success or a failure. Developing a daily script organizes your attention into the most important and strategic activities. It's easy to be overwhelmed by large goals so you need a way to break it down into parts that you can focus on in increments of time. This enables you to get in the zone for 90-120 minutes at a time, hopefully for two or three time blocks each day. If completed step-by-step, each day, week, month, and year, you will complete your big goal. It really comes down to your daily script.

The final step is to review your weekly goals/tasks and decide which of the five or six days that week you will focus on each task. It may require several of the days to complete a particular task, which is okay. Take the time and build your daily scripts for the week, making sure you have slotted the completion of each goal for the week into a day. My personal preference is to get up early on a Sunday morning to review my past week, review upcoming goals/tasks that need to be completed from the monthly goal plan, and then schedule in each day's tasks right down to the time of day when I will complete each. This enables me to rest easy knowing I'm set up for success each day, my big goals are being acted upon, and when I sit down at my desk on Monday morning, I can go right into the zone and get amazing work done.

One final thought on building a daily script that works for you is to consider your chronotype. Dr. Michael Brues, author of the book *The Power of When: Discover Your Chronotype—and the Best Time to Eat Lunch, Ask for a Raise, Have Sex, Write a Novel, Take Your Meds, and More*, suggests that when we do things matters based on our chronotype. Dr. Brues explains in his book that a chronotype is the propensity to sleep during a certain time period. He categorizes people into four chronotypes: the bear, wolf, lion, and dolphin. I'm a lion, meaning I get up early with plenty of energy and I am sharpest in the morning. Nearly every word of this book was written prior to lunch time. You can go to his quiz at **www.thepowerofwhenquiz. com** and learn your chronotype. Once you do, build your script to mesh with your rhythms rather than forcing yourself into a rhythm that you will fight.

Weekly Planning Session

This is your time to get up early one weekend morning and complete a weekly planning process. It takes about an hour to review your quarterly and monthly goals, establish what needs to be done for the coming week based on your past work and any changes due to new information, and fill out day scripts for each day of the coming week. You will come to value this time and the feelings of accomplishment from simply setting your week up for success. What you have done is set yourself up for complete focus each and every day because you aren't wasting cognitive energy and bandwidth on figuring out what you will do or what you need to find to complete a task. It's all planned and all you have to do is sit down and do the work in front of you, knowing it's building toward the successful realization of your worthwhile goals.

You might be thinking I'm a bit neurotic and this seems like a lot of work. Well, let me say this first: You're reading a performance book so of course work is involved. Secondly, if you want to do or experience the things that the top 1% performers experience, then you must be willing to do what 99% of others won't do. All of the elite performing individuals have some form of an intense planning process and goal orientation that goes well beyond anything I've seen "normal" people do. This isn't a value judgement on people in general, I'm simply sharing observations on those who have made a personal choice to do something extraordinary with their life and went to extraordinary means to achieve the life of their dreams. The choice is yours.

How Goal Stacking Relates to Flow

The foundation of a robust personal or organizational goal management system is that goals come from a place of clarity. You have defined your transformative purpose, created a vision and mission, and outlined core values, all aligned with a destination as defined by your long-term goals. The rest of the process is simple execution to help you take the day-to-day steps needed to reach those goals. What I'm suggesting in this book is that you harness the power of getting in the zone to accelerate the realization of your goals and life purpose rather than trying to work harder and longer.

If flow is the answer, you need to organize your life to get more of it to realize its powerful effects. The number-one focus must be to manage attention and direct it at the most important goals consistently over time to gain the power of compounding. To compound, you need sustained motivation, sustained energy, and sustained focus over time. Every chapter of this book has focused on improving one of those three drivers of compounding success through getting in the zone. Total absorption into a task, the balancing of the challenges/skills ratio, having clear goals, developing and demonstrating grit and increased performance through flow, and feedback are supported by a system to progressively clear and reduce the scope of your goals into daily tasks. Additionally, a goal management system that works off a daily script lowers cognitive load and distraction. By making the investment in a clear goal-setting process such as this one, you're setting yourself up to get in the zone at will each and every day. Repeating your flow day schedule, with all of your automated routines day after day, will compound into massive results.

My hope is that this process will be motivational and encouraging. The concept of cause and effect says actions taken today will lead to a corresponding effect in the future. Compounding strategic actions day after day lead to stacked positive consequences. If you gain clarity, add in strategic goal setting, take daily action steps seriously toward your most important goals, all while getting in the zone, you have set the stage to do the impossible. Here's the Greatness Formula for you to write someplace that you'll see it every day:

Priority Work x Flow x Time Compounded = Greatness

Before you move on to Chapter 12, sit with a legal pad and a pen and just let yourself dream. Think about what you could accomplish if you implemented the principles in this book and applied the Greatness Formula. Consider the opportunities if you could prioritize your work, do the things you need to do to get in the zone consistently, and see the results from each day in flow compounded into extraordinary results. Visualize this. Feel the emotions as you see it in your mind—how does it feel? What kind of impact can you have on others if you realize this dream? What can you do for your family, church, or a non-profit organization that you love if you can perform at this higher level? Invest some time to write out what you see and feel, while visualizing it and use this journal entry to fuel your inner fire to become an elite performer.

Implementation Checklist

✓ Build on your purpose and core values by creating your personal goal stack.
✓ Enroll in Tiger's Get Into the Zone online course for in-depth instruction on how to create this performance foundation. Go to www.tigerpi.com/online-courses

Chapter 12:

You²: The Power of Group Flow

> *"One source of frustration in the workplace is the frequent mismatch between what people must do and what people can do. When what they must do exceeds their capabilities, the result is anxiety. When what they must do falls short of their capabilities, the result is boredom. But when the match is just right, the results can be glorious. This is the essence of flow."*
>
> —DANIEL PINK, author

In Diane Ransom's *Entrepreneur* magazine article, "Finding Success by Putting Company Culture First," she reviews the cultural practices at Google, Patagonia, and Zappos that promote flow within their organizations. Patagonia provides ample time for recovery, promotion of the challenge/skills balance, novelty, and autonomy by allowing staff to surf, mountain bike, climb and travel frequently during their workday. Google has culture clubs that bring people together to talk, promoting flow. Google also has 20% time, which is time each week that employees can invest in a project idea they have, promoting a growth mindset, challenge/skills balance, and autonomy. Zappos instills risk into the employment decision. Each staff member who stays on as an employee has forgone $4,000 to be there. Additionally, Zappos provides over 40 on-site classes for ongoing education, which promotes the challenge/skills balance, autonomy, and growth mindset as well.

The purpose of this chapter is to introduce the concept of group flow. Up to this point, the book has been exclusively about individual flow and how to set your life up to get in the zone at will. But most people also work for organizations. When individuals can get in the zone, there's a positive impact on their performance and well-being, which ultimately funnels into their organization. Team flow is capable of producing extraordinary results and improving the collective well-being of employees across the entire organization. When a leader can train individuals to get in the zone and create the culture, leadership, and process to promote group flow, the organization is positioned to seize opportunities most organizations can't muster the focus to pursue. This chapter introduces team flow and some of its thought leaders. This will be far from a complete presentation on how to scale getting in the zone but Tiger Performance Institute has additional resources for you to investigate if you want to take your team's flow leadership to the next level.

Group Flow Defined

It's appropriate at this junction to establish a clear definition of group flow. In their 2016 book, *The Application of Team Flow Theory in Flow Experience: Empirical Research and Applications*, authors Jeff Van Den Hout, Orin Davis, and Bob Walgrave concluded from their research that team flow is characterized by all team members being completely involved in their common activities as part of a collaboration toward the common purpose or goal. Team flow is when individuals experience flow while performing their tasks within a team context. Team Flow has three core aspects:

1) It's an individual team member who experiences the mental state of flow by executing his/her personal task.

2) The team member derives flow from the team dynamic, which is structured by a collective ambition that set shared goals (team and personal), high skill integration, open communication, safety, and mutual commitment.

3) Team members share a dynamic that reflects a state of flow as a whole, which is characterized by five specific components: trust, focus, a sense of unity, a sense of joint progress, and a shared identity (that expresses the collective ambition).

The authors concluded that occurrence of team flow leads to a meaningful experience and satisfaction for the individual team members, which is probably stronger than experiencing solitary flow. In other words, people like group flow even more than getting in the zone by themselves because it's a shared experience producing energy and positive feelings

Group Flow Triggers

The leader in group flow research is Dr. Keith Sawyer, a professor at the University of North Carolina in Chapel Hill, who in his 2015 paper, "Group Flow and Group Genius," wrote that the spontaneous collaboration of group creativity and improvisation led to group flow. Group flow in organizations can be harnessed to drive optimal function in teams, leading to improved organizational performance. Dr. Sawyer's research has led to the development of what he calls, "The Ten Conditions of Group Flow," which can be viewed as flow triggers for teams. The right kind of leader can learn and engineer these conditions or triggers into the culture of their teams or organizations.

10 Conditions of Group Flow:

1. Complete concentration—workspace privacy, distraction management, and focus
2. Autonomy—sense of control and empowerment to decide or act
3. Close listening—listening to understand, not to respond
4. Communication—frequent interaction about expectations relating to vision and individual contributions toward organizational vision
5. Equal participation—everyone has ability to contribute and they do

6. Blending of egos—shared vision, shared buy-in, team orientation—no jerks

7. Shared goals—greater purpose than the individual and seeing progress on goals

8. Shared risk and unpredictability—potential for failure exists for the team

9. Familiarity—team gains understanding of each other and how each works

10. Positive no—rather than a "shut-down" no, use "okay, and" to draw out more thinking and understand their perspective and idea

When several if not all of these triggers or conditions can be designed into the team dynamic, it can lead to substantial gains in team productivity, creativity, and learning. When teams function at this level, friction of any kind is reduced, progress is accelerated, and the organization is optimized, not just the individual. Success at the team or organizational level of this magnitude is rare but achievable with the right form of leadership.

Author Daniel Pink in his book, *Drive: The Surprising Truth About What Motivates Us*, offers a simpler version of how to build a high-performing culture, which in my view, produces group flow. Pink establishes three drivers of an intrinsically motivating environment in the workplace:

- Purpose—a shared "why" that has organizational buy-in at all levels
- Path to mastery—a road map for each job role to gain mastery
- Empowerment—once trained, each person has the opportunity to exercise control

A quick review clearly shows several components of flow are encompassed in Pink's framework for creating a performance culture. First, clarity of direction and agreement within the team is present. Intrinsic motivation is foundational to flow because there needs to be a growth process present collectively in all members of the team. This leads to a growth mindset necessary for mastery. Mastery also promotes hitting the sweet spot of the challenge/skills ratio required to move from the struggle phase through the release phase into the flow phase of the flow cycle. Additionally, empowerment is another word for autonomy. People crave autonomy once their skills are up to the challenge and without it, they become bored and disengaged, which blocks their contribution to group flow. Shared agreement on vision blends egos, fosters good communication, facilitates "yes" thinking, and concentrates attention on the right priorities.

Leadership and Flow

There is one simple question for leaders to ponder when considering flow: How do you migrate your personal ability to get in the zone to those you lead within the organization? The answer has exciting possibilities because when a leader gets this right, exponential growth can occur in an organization, much like the example from the sage asking the king to double the number of grains of rice for each place on the chessboard. While Keith Sawyer and Daniel Pink's work on the conditions or triggers for group flow are helpful, they are incomplete in terms of providing a framework from which a leader can attempt to scale flow across their organization or team.

In their book, *Flow: Get Everyone Moving in The Right Direction and Loving It,* Ted and Andrew Kallman developed three decades' worth of research from hands-on, practical application and created the best frameworks I have seen for scaling flow in teams and organizations. While it's elegantly simple, it's complicated and difficult work to actually accomplish. My goal is to introduce it here and encourage you to read their book or visit Tiger Performance Institute 's website for more information on now to fully develop organizational flow among those you lead.

The essence of the flow model is that it starts with vision. Wisdom from the Bible in the book of Proverbs chapter 29, verse 18 (NIV) states, "Where there is no revelation (vision), people cast off restraint; but blessed is the one who heeds wisdom's instruction." Vision is an organization's "to be" statement of intent about a planned future achievement or reality. Achieving flow organizationally demands vision be clear, simple, and memorable from the top to the bottom within the organization. If vision is absent, as the Bible states, anarchy reigns, preventing the achievement of goals.

The next part of the model requires a clear statement of the mission, or the definition of the business the organization is in. Business is a descriptive term—a school, religious organization, or a non-profit are in the business of something that requires definition. Once the mission is defined, a purpose statement is developed. This is the higher meaning that the team is working toward—it's the collective "why" of the organization. Next, leadership should work with a select group of team members to develop organizational core values. These values describe what the company stands for, what is right behavior in the organization, and what will be the standard from which future strategy, goals, and behavior are measured against. Finally, clear goals and objectives need to be established to provide a road map for team members to follow and act.

In summary, the Flow Formula to scale flow across an organization is:

Flow Formula = Vision + Right People + 4D Model

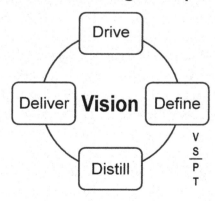

Starting at the right with "Define," leadership defines the vision, mission, purpose, values, as well as the strategies and objectives in a way that's clear. This isn't completely top-down as the next step in the process, "Distill," is crucial for buy-in. In the distillation phase, all of the vision and job expectations definitions are distilled into agreement with the team, therefore the team does exercise some input into the process and through distillation, agreement is gained and buy-in cemented. Upon achieving clarity of vision and distilled agreement, the team is in the position to deliver results. Without results, people are working at cross purposes and chaos ensues. Finally, in the 4D model, leadership needs to communicate 10 times more than it thinks necessary to drive the organization through each step of achieving its vision.

The VSPS on the lower right-hand side of the model stands for Vision, Strategy, People, and Tasks. Vision and strategy are at the executive level while people and tasks are at the team or individual level. The top two use the language of leadership while the bottom two use the language of management. This illustrates why it can be difficult to build understanding between the two levels and why many projects, product launches, and goal management systems seeking to drive results fail.

Leadership's role is to use this model as a process at the enterprise level and for every level below enterprise. For each team within the organization, each department, division, product, and product line, this process of applying the Vision + Right People + 4D model should be implemented. The goal is to align the individual and group vision, mission, purpose, values, and goals with and in support of the organization's vision, mission, purpose, values, and goals. When this is achieved, organizational flow occurs.

There are multiple means to organize and manage companies and non-profit organizations. Some use traditional organizational charts with command and control structures, often referred to as traditional management. However, there are multiple project management systems and branded approaches. A major trend the past decade has been to embrace "agile" or "scrum" management philosophy, which seeks to approach driving results through the autonomous, self-organizing, and self-directed teams. Each approach has varying success/failure rates but regardless of the approach, at best nearly 60% of strategy initiatives, change programs, or projects fail, according the authors of *The Nehemiah Effect*, Ted and Andrew Kallman. The challenge with these approaches is that they tend to create disconnects from the teams and executive leadership. By applying the model above, it transcends all approaches, to unify the organization around shared vision, mission, purpose, values, and goals. In other words, the Flow Formula is methodology agnostic. The Flow Formula is easy to integrate into whatever methods or frameworks you may already be using to achieve the goals of your organization or team. The Flow Formula is utilized above the various project management methods to bring down friction and get people working together by getting them into the zone as a team and individually.

"There is also a collective version of a flow state known as group flow. That is what happens when a bunch of people enter the zone together."

—STEVEN KOTLER,
author of Stealing Fire.

Family and Group Flow

Research suggests flow in families is real and something you should pursue. Not only is it good for the well-being of the family, but it also lays the groundwork for your children to build the traits and habits into their lives to enable them to get in the zone later in life. In the *Scandinavian Journal of Hospitality and Tourism*, a study by Jacob Larsen and R. Kirkegaard titled, "Family Flow: The Pleasures of Being Together in a Holiday Home," revealed the benefits of taking a holiday together and promoting family flow. Based on 26 in-depth whole-family interviews with Danish, German, and Norwegian families on holiday in a Danish holiday home this article focused on the pleasures of being together from parents' and children's perspectives. The article illustrates that the social experience of family holiday and special moments of togetherness during vacation in a holiday home promote the twin pleasures of excitement and relaxation. A family dynamic of interrelated pleasures creates a "family flow," leading to an optimal holiday experience for both parents and children, which contributes to the well-being during a family holiday.

As this chapter comes to a close, I thought I would share some research I found on flow in the family. It's profitable to invest in performance enhancement to reach your work goals and provide well for the family, however, if that's all you focus on, you'll be left with feelings of emptiness or regret if you lose your family. I've discussed that part of learning to get in the zone is learning to balance cycles of work with recovery. Forms of recovery can be primary flow activities or activities you enjoy that you can get into the zone while doing. These support work-based flow because the more flow you get, the more flow you get. A wise person plans these recovery activities with the family in mind.

Developing Flow in Children

Mihaly Czikszentmihalyi, in his seminal book *Flow: The Psychology of Optimal Experience*, suggests that early childhood influences likely contribute to whether a person will or will not easily experience flow. Evidence suggests how parents interact with their child will have a lasting effect on the kind of person that child grows up to be.

The family environment that is optimal for promoting flow experiences is what I'm calling

The Five Cs of Family Flow:

1. Clarity—your child feels like they understand parental expectations
2. Centering—a child's perception that their parent is interested in what they're doing in the present, rather than preoccupation with only the future
3. Choice—child perceives they have multiple options, not being forced to choose their parent's preference
4. Commitment—a trusting environment that allows the child to put down defenses
5. Challenge—the parents are dedicated to providing increasingly challenging or complex opportunities for their child

The presence of these five characteristics creates what Czikszetmihalyi calls "the autotelic family context." This provides an ideal setting for learning how to enjoy life and the five characteristics parallel to the dimensions of flow. Children who grow up in settings that facilitate clarity of goals, feedback, feelings of control, concentration on task at hand, intrinsic motivation, and challenge will generally have a better chance to order their lives so as to make flow possible.

If you have children in the home, consider the list above and think of creative ways to put challenges in front of your kids through sports, music, reading, the arts, or other school activities. Be clear about what your family stands for and your expectations of them as members of the family and of society. Avoid the "always about the future" orientation that most parents have. This was a challenge for me. In my desire to help my kids become productive adults, I spent too much time treating them like they were adults rather than kids. Something my wife did very well was giving our kids choices. Sometimes they didn't want as many as she provided them, but they always knew they were being empowered to make choices. Finally, make it safe in your home to experiment, fail, recover, and get better as a result. Create a stable environment where you keep your commitments and your kids trust that you have their backs no matter what. When you can create this kind of culture in the home, you set up your kids to be peak performers of the future.

In our family we decided when our son was 7 years old to attend a game at all 30 major league baseball stadiums. Our daughter was 9 at the time and not a baseball fan. We made sure to tour each city, giving her an opportunity to choose activities, while our son was more than content to see all the games and stadiums. This activity spanned eleven years and incorporated several of the five C's. My wife started a dessert business with our daughter when she entered junior high that also incorporated most of the five C's. Finally, when my daughter experienced faltering confidence at acceptance into Baylor University's University Scholars honors program, I made the commitment to her to read nearly 100 great texts or classic works of literature with her over the five years of her program. The point is, you can find your own ways to connect with and challenge your kids to promote flow in the family.

Implementation Checklist

✓ If you are in position of leadership, which 1-2 group flow triggers could you implement today to foster team flow? Consider this a topic of a team meeting to discuss to determine which triggers would most excite and motivate your team.

✓ If you are a parent, assess the Five C's of Family Flow and begin to implement one of the five today.

Chapter 13:

Learning to Fly: Your Opportunity

"The illiterate of the 21st century will not be those who cannot read and write, but those who cannot learn, unlearn, and relearn."

—ALVIN TOFFLER,

futurist

This book began with the story of the sage and the king and how the sage used the power of exponentials to become the wealthiest man in the world. You are living in an exponential age of change, the age of the Great Restructuring, as MIT Professors Brynjolfsson and MacAfee suggested in their book of the same title. In many ways this age has been happening while people go about their business unnoticed, barely detected. There are steady improvements in life, such as faster or higher quality internet speed and improved experiences on websites, but the big, game-changing types of change that impact our employment and businesses hadn't shown up... Until the Pandemic of 2020.

The advances in technology became apparent as consumers stayed home and work patterns changed dramatically, exposing types of work, industries, and businesses with business models that won't thrive going forward. It's also shown who some of the winners will be when it comes to longevity. My point is not to discuss winners and losers during this time of duress, but more to demonstrate the massive change from the convergence of accelerating technologies that's beginning to show up. We're seemingly entering a period of multiple tipping points of mass adoption to these new technologies that will in turn lead to unprecedented developments with implications for our everyday lives, businesses, and work. A sampling of why we aren't ready include:

- Much of the technology changes will be good and improve the quality of life. I'm no Luddite; I embrace change as good for the most part. However, the picture of this new world, as put forth by Ray Kurzweil and other futurists, suggest that life will require much more going forward if we want to thrive and live the kind of life that's coveted. A reading of the data suggests large swaths of society are unprepared for what's unfolding: 77% of adults suffer from stress to the point that they experience physical symptoms
- A whopping 6 in 10 adults suffer from a chronic disease, with a stunning 4 in 10 having two or more chronic diseases.
- Nearly all HR professionals say there is an epidemic of burnout in the workplace.
- As a nation at work, we are massively distracted by gadgets and digital communication.

These statistics are stunning as they highlight that the majority of adults in the U.S. aren't well. The numbers suggest many fall into each of these categories, meaning they are experiencing massive interference, preventing them from feeling and working their best. Because people are stressed, sick, burned out, and distracted, they aren't in a position to learn, unlearn, and relearn, deeming them the 21st-century illiterates that Toffler refers to. Toffler is saying that if you can't learn in the 21st century, it's akin to not being able to read in the 20th century. This is a powerful statement as the blitzkrieg of change requires rapid adaption. Learning is the antidote to change—it's a prerequisite of adaptation.

Taking this idea of learning as a core skill for adaption, Cal Newport, professor at Georgetown University, outlined in his book *Deep Work* that we need two core skills to thrive in this exponential era:

1. The ability to quickly master hard things
2. The ability to produce at an elite level, in terms of both quality and speed

Your ability to observe the massive change coming, understand it, think through your own strategy to adapt to it, and then learn, re-skill, and produce are dependent upon possessing the physiological and psychological make-up to take on this challenge. If you are filled with toxic rather than good stress, you can't think properly and will likely suffer from mental health problems. If you have uncontrolled chronic disease or are living in such a way that you're on the road to it, then this will limit your capacity. If you work in an environment that's toxic, offers little reward in relation to our efforts, then you're on your way to burnout. Your best work cannot come out of this sort of environment. Lastly, if you live on your devices and fill time with checking email and surfing the internet, the best you can do is low-value, shallow work as Newport says.

What you need is a better version of yourself. The answer is not to work harder; running faster will not solve the problem. High-value work rarely emerges from rushing or working at a frantic pace. In fact, more hours are proven to offer diminishing productivity returns and focuses on the wrong thing: Input rather than what is actually produced. Working longer, harder, and faster only makes you sicker than you already are. It will only serve to lower your wellbeing as our relationships suffer and mental health issues emerge from the overwork and stress of relational distress. If working harder, more diligently, and at greater speed isn't the answer, then what is? You need to step back, get very strategic, and re-engineer your life to get into flow. Getting in the zone is the recipe for overcoming the monumental changes arriving at our doorsteps and the secret to turning our current work habits into a healthier approach to living.

Your goal needs to be deep work, the label coined by Professor Newport and defined as, "Professional activities performed in a state of distraction-free concentration that push your cognitive capabilities to their limit. These efforts create new value, improve your skill, and hard to replicate."

To produce deep work, the answer is to get in the zone. This optimal state of consciousness is where your cognitive capabilities are pushed to the limit, where you learn, grow, and produce new insights and work that has real value. The zone is real—it has a neurobiological signature that has been validated by quality research. Getting in the zone is good for you because of what is required before you can get into this state. It requires personal growth, hobbies, and recovery. You must learn to cycle your work pattern between focus and recovery throughout each day and other time periods as well. Decluttering, simplifying, and ordering your life are required. Clarity, purpose, and defeating distraction are prerequisites of getting in the zone. It's clear that these and the other changes outlined in this book will enable you to optimize your psychology and physiology and improve your overall sense of well-being. To be a flow hacker and operate in an optimal state daily, you have to live by a set of habits that are both really good for you and that will empower you to do deep, high-value work and live a better life. As you consistently live in this manner you will become a super version of who you are today.

Return on Your Flow Investment

So, what's the actual impact of getting in the zone? If it hasn't been researched and quantified in some way, then it's only a speculation. In a study run in Australia at the University of Sydney, research subjects were presented with an exceptionally tricky brain teaser—the kind that requires a deep creative insight to solve. When flow was induced artificially, researchers saw a 430% improvement in creative problem solving. The Flow Genome Project (Kotler's Organization) has studies revealing that individuals from a far-ranging field—everyone from entrepreneurs to scientists to writers—report being seven times (i.e., 700%) more creative in flow. Harvard's Teresa Amiable discovered that not only are people more creative in flow, but they also report being more creative three days after a flow state, suggesting that flow doesn't just heighten creativity in the moment, it heightens it over the long haul. In other words, being in flow actually trains us to be more creative.

In a Defense Advanced Research Projects Agency (DARPA) study on accelerated learning in flow, it found that soldiers who were induced into the flow state improved learning speed and mastered new skills by 490%. Neuroscientists from DARPA and Advanced Brain Monitoring carried out this test by inducing the flow state through neurofeedback. Neurofeedback is "a form of biofeedback" in which a person responds to a display of their own brain waves or other electrical activity of the nervous system. As they continue training, the brain learns from the feedback to reregulate brain wave frequencies into an optimal range, a range that is conducive to getting in the zone. Neurofeedback is a shortcut in the process of preparing for a high-flow lifestyle.

The *Harvard Business Review* cites a 10-year study conducted by McKinsey where top executives reported being five times more productive in flow. The study shared that if a person or team spent Monday in flow, they would get as much done as their peers do in a week. McKinsey researchers reveal that if you could increase the time that you spend in flow by 15-20%, overall workplace productivity would almost double. "In all our studies of extreme performance improvement," says John Hagel, co-founder of Deloitte's Center for the Edge, "The people and organizations who covered the most distance in the shortest time were always the ones who were tapping into passion and finding flow."

A *Forbes* article revealed that time spent in flow should be the number one metric. Especially for roles that require a lot of brainpower, such as software programming, engineering, marketing, or writing. These roles demand deep concentration—getting in the zone. Unfortunately, most knowledge workers are constantly interrupted during the day with meetings, emails, texts, or colleagues who want to talk. These interruptions that move us out of "flow state" increase research and development cycle times and costs dramatically. Studies have shown that each time a flow state is disrupted, it takes 15 minutes to get back into flow, if you can get back at all. And programmers who work in the top quartile of proper (i.e., uninterrupted) work environments are several times more productive than those who do not.

The evidence is clear: Getting in the zone is real and it improves your results. Think about what a 500% improvement in your productivity can mean for the achievement of your goals. It would enable you to redefine what's possible in your work career. What new advances could you make in your work if you could learn 490% faster or amp up your creativity by 430%? Armed with these new powers, you can confidently look at the future and know you will thrive by learning and adapting positively to change. Logic suggests your results will be better than what you're experiencing today and offers an exciting set of possibilities to consider for your future. The research should encourage and motivate you to make the changes necessary to get in the zone.

Your Opportunity

This book has provided you with a road map to become the best version of yourself by learning to design your life and adopt a set of habits that will enable you to enter flow on a daily basis, at will. Ideas are a dime a dozen, and those who implement ideas are priceless. If you follow this road map, you'll prepare your nervous system, brain, body, and mindset to achieve flow when you need to get great work done. The answer to the 21st century's challenge is deep work done in a state of flow. It's not to rush and press on; no, you want to actually do less and produce more. Only getting in the zone will enable you to unlock the key to this paradox. I believe this quote from Cal Newport is a motivational challenge that you need to push forward, "Our work culture's shift toward the shallow is exposing a massive economic and personal opportunity for the few who recognize the potential of resisting this trend and prioritizing depth."

Newport's quote says so much about the general direction of the herd and your opportunity to do the opposite. In a sense, the few who choose to take this route in life and develop a passion for depth and do deep work in flow will reap disproportionate rewards. So, my encouragement to you is to take this challenge. Be one of the few who decides to take the passionate path of elite performance and enjoy giant-sized results. For those who do, you can enjoy the thought that you did your part to prepare and provide for your family through this next wave of change under your watch. Finally, think and consider how you can leverage the success you enjoy into positively impacting others in the world as well.

Implementation Checklist

✓ Decide today if you have a big vision you want to pursue.
✓ Define that vision clearly on paper and visualize achieving it, noting the emotion and how much it motivates you to take action.
✓ Partner with Tiger Performance Institute to accelerate your progress toward your vision!

Chapter 14:

Next Steps For You

"There is a time when one must decide either to risk everything to fulfill one's dreams or sit for the rest of one's life in the backyard."

—EARL NIGHTINGALE,
author & national radio host

This quote by Nightingale is one that I'm sure I read and pondered on sometime during the '90s when I was trying to decide whether or not I would leave my prosperous and relatively secure career as a corporate banker. Ultimately, I did decide to pursue my dream of starting a business. I recall the day we finished packing up two box trucks with our possessions to move to Appleton, Wisconsin. My best friend, Dr. Tom, and his wife and their two girls stood with my wife and our two little kids as I locked up the doors and prepared to leave on the six-hour journey to begin our new life. I was leaving a week early with my brother, dad, and my wife's uncle to set up our new home and start on the new store. As I pulled away, I looked in the mirror and watched them wave as I made the turn and my new adventure began. The key here is that I was able to move from abstract thought (creating a vision and plan) to implementation by taking action. To enter the zone and achieve amazing performance, you also need to move from the information and inspiration of this book to implementation.

Fast forward 21 years. As I left the business I had started all those years ago, I was burned out and hurting. I fell into a pattern of running so hard, ignoring my health and my wife that I didn't finish well. Through the process of recovering my health, energy, and restoring my most important relationships, the idea for Tiger Performance Institute emerged. Peak performance is not only about ambition and success, it's also about learning how to design your life for performance that enhances your well-being and relationships. My passion today is to help people avoid the pattern that played out in my life. If you're already in a pattern of unending stress, living a rushed and hectic existence, the good news is that you can change. If you struggle with never-ending time pressure, you can transform you daily existence, not just improve it.

Tiger Performance Institute operates with a very simple two-word vision: Optimize performance. We want all of our clients to learn how to use flow and a few basic tools to improve their health and ability to manage stress to drive massive gains in performance at work while enriching their lives outside of their careers. We know that as you learn to eliminate some things, add others into your life, build new habits, and learn to get in the zone, your performance significantly improves and the quality of your life gets better, too. This isn't an easy process— it requires work, experimentation, and adjustment until you find the unique combination that best works for you.

The iterative process of elevating your performance is relatively straightforward and simple, but simple is not always easy. We understand this and have curated a simple path to transformation for anyone willing to start. A phrase I often use within our organization and with our clients is, "If you want top 5% results, you have to be willing to do what 95% of the general population is unwilling to do on a consistent basis." Being in the top 5% is not about being better than others in the sense of a prideful or haughty view; being in the top 5% represents a mindset more than some precise definition. We emphasize that performance and success is based on your individual definition of success.

For those who choose to work with us at Tiger Performance Institute, the journey begins with a three-part course online on how to get in the zone. It covers every area you need to learn and redesign your life to live a high-flow lifestyle. In our experience, clients that begin with education have a better experience in our coaching programs, and as a result, we have eliminated the option of skipping education to get to the coaching programs. However, because we know information alone doesn't lead to transformation for everyone, we've designed specific coaching programs to help you implement what you've learned in this book as well as our "Get In The Zone" online courses. Coaching is a proven way to amplify the results of new knowledge by improving application and new habit formation through dialogue and accountability provided by a coach. Additionally, we have designed two advanced coaching programs that help you establish a physiological foundation to get in the zone at will, transform your sleep and ability to manage stress, and a physician-designed health optimization program.

I want to thank you for investing the time, concentration, and effort to read this book all the way through. At the end of reading a book I often feel excitement from learning something new, only to see the passion fade as time goes by and I get into the next book. I realize there is a lot of information provided here, which can present a challenge to implement even a small portion of the suggestions offered. However, the stakes are high. Don't miss the opportunity of this moment after being educated on the broader trends affecting your life and making an investment in learning so much. I hope to meet you one day on your peak performance journey.

To take that next best step go to www.tigernpi.com and explore our website and consider joining our team by signing up for a course to begin your journey of unleashing the peak performer that lies within you. It's just waiting to come out and you have 100% control of when and if it does.

Acknowledgements

When an author writes a book, it's an exercise in discipline and persistence. Early on in a project a sense of overwhelm can creep in a moment's notice, like changing weather patterns on Lake Michigan near my home. My wife of 33 years, who has endured the ebbs and flows of my corporate career, the launch and growth of a retail business and the recent start up of Tiger, knows well my patterns and weaknesses. On our daily walks through the neighborhood and into our favorite wooded paths with our dog Bella, she would listen to me go on and on about an aspect of my research or how I was struggling with how to present an idea. Throughout the process, she listened and encouraged me to keep going, seeing the vision for the book and how it could impact others. Thank you Heidi for listening and being the encouragement you are in all the endeavors I get myself into.

I want to thank our team at Tiger Performance Institute. Dr. Matthew McNamee, NMD is a brilliant clinician with a vision to work with patients proactively, before they present medical conditions. Dr. Michael Mannino, Ph.D. for your incredible depth of knowledge in the field of neuroscience and peak performance, you inspire our team and grow our knowledge of this exciting field. To Lance VanTine and Collin Adams who coach our clients each day. You are mature beyond your years and bring passion and deep expertise to your work. Thank you for how you put all of yourself into each of your clients and into our vision at Tiger. I appreciate the skill and calm demeanor of our principal technology architect, Colton Nixon who has built and continues to build a world-class back end to our business at Tiger, to ensure the best possible experience for our clients. Thank you, Colton for your expertise and tireless effort to do your part in building out our vision to optimize performance.

If you read my writing before my amazing editor put her skilled mind to work, you wouldn't have enjoyed this book as much! Kelsey Turek has the unique ability to enhance the author's message while keeping the book in the author's voice. Kelsey took the challenge of keeping up with my pace as I utilized the principles shared in this book to write the entire book in a flow state and shorten the creative cycle. Thank you, Kelsey. You made this book much better and I'm looking forward to writing many more books with you by my side.

I made two new friends in Serbia while putting the finishing touches on this book, Nada and Lily who created the book cover and produced the look and feel of the book interior respectively. Thank you, ladies for your great skill and enthusiasm for the book. I look forward to many more books with you as well.

I also want to thank coach Patrick Chambers at Penn State University. You gave my start-up a chance when few would, to come along side you and some of your players to utilize the tools our company deploys and that are shared in this book. I've enjoyed getting to know you and see first-hand, what an excellent leader, father and husband you are. I count it as one of the great joys in my life to get to know you, your team, and your family.

To all our individual and clinic clients, I want to say that without you, there is not Tiger Performance Institute and no book. You entrust us each day to optimize your performance and we do not take that for granted, thank you.

About the

Author

S teve Adams is a former corporate banker and veteran entrepreneur. His passion lies in building and scaling organizations through disciplined execution, direct-response marketing and culture that leads to extraordinary client experiences. Steve grew up in Lansing, Michigan as the son of an auto worker. He went on to university and became the first college graduate and MBA in his family.

Steve's first career was in banking in Detroit and Grand Rapids, Michigan (1986—1996). At the bank he moved through the retail, then corporate banking divisions becoming one of the top producing bankers in an $80 billion international bank. He later managed a $1BN portfolio for another bank in Green Bay, WI (1998—1999). His last role in banking was Regional President of a bank (1999—2002) in Michigan at age 35.

After banking, Steve's first venture was a retail organization inside a new franchised pet superstore concept (1996—2017). Steve, his partners and team innovated and developed many approaches which later were adapted nationally by the franchisor. This organization ultimately ended up growing to over 40 units in 6 states with approximately 750 employees and revenues of approximately $100mm.

Currently, Steve is engaged in developing a peak performance company called Tiger Performance Institute (www.tigernpi.com), serving individuals seeking elite-performance, addiction treatment centers, and major university athletics programs.

Steve is also the author of the book *Passionate Entrepreneur*, published through Advantage Publishing.

In 2008 Steve founded International Business as Mission (www.ibam.org), an international non-profit providing entrepreneurial training and start-up funding in developing nations.

Tiger Performance Institute

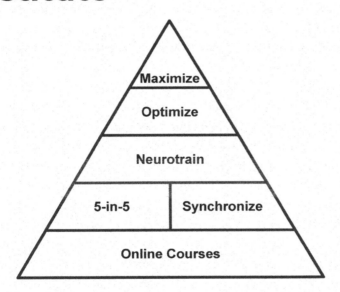

Tiger Performance Institute optimizes individual performance through publishing, online courses, individual coaching, biofeedback, and medical optimization programs. All programs focus on helping individuals' access and perform in flow states, multiplying performance by 500% or more, while vastly improving creativity, problem solving and learning speed.

Tiger's programs are designed to for the individual to work through a process from basic peak performance learning all the way through to Tiger's health optimization programs Optimize and Maximize.

Our online course, Accelerate Your Growth starts your peak performance journey, teaching basic principles in peak performance, while using neuroscience to form new habits that will lay the groundwork for future performance gains.

Get into the Zone is a comprehensive and highly researched course on developing the ability to work in flow states where research has validated 500% performance gains. The world is changing faster than ever, machine learning is requiring more of people than ever to remain employed. Getting into the zone, not running harder is the answer to this new era we work in.

5/5 Performance Coaching is our next step for those who took our Accelerate Your Growth course. In this program a personal certified performance coach will interact with you on a daily basis for 5 weeks to form new habits and gain extreme clarity around your future goals. Pre and post assessment are included, providing data to validate your progress.

Synchronize is our biofeedback coaching program that will transform your sleep and redefine your relationship with stress. Heart rate variability improvement through heart coherence breathing is the cornerstone of this program. Benefits include improved immune function, greater calm under pressure, improved focus, and greater resilience. It is foundational to performing in the zone.

Neurotrain is our signature neurofeedback program. Everyone has dysregulated brain wave activity which leads to behavioral challenges that act as interference to peak performance. Neurotrain uses spaced repetition learning via video games, videos, or audio to train your brain to re-regulate its wave activity. Benefits include greater calm, less anxiety, more focus, and better mood and sleep.

Optimize is our first-level precision medicine program which begins your journey to elite performance health. Our physician reviews your medical history in depth, administers a DNA test and then provides feedback that enables you to target, with precision certain habits that will best line up with your DNA blueprint.

Maximize is Tiger's concierge medicine program for those clients who seek the ultimate in peak performance. This client has gone through our courses and coaching programs and seeks to work with a performance-minded and educated doctor. Concierge medicine includes an extensive annual physical exam, a detailed annual medical plan, quarterly coaching calls with your health coach and anytime access to our doctor.

For more information about Tiger programs go to **www.tigerpi.com** and request a free consult with the author for more information.

FREE Checklist:
From "Burnout, Distraction and Stress to Prosperity"

- **10 ways to do your best work**, any one of which can protect your income.
- **How to achieve more, without time management** (hint: it's time expansion)
- **Over 251 books and articles on Peak Performance boiled down to 2 pages**
- It's the ultimate productivity tool. Don't miss out ...Get Your Free Checklist
- **Go to www./tigerpi.com/checklist**

Bibliography

Introduction

https://www.stress.org/stress-research, The American Institute of Stress, 7.8.2014.

Brynjolfsson, Erik, and Andrew McAfee. 2011. *Race Against the Machine: How the Digital Revolution Is Accelerating Innovation, Driving Productivity, and Irreversibly Transforming Employment and the Economy.* Brynjolfsson and McAfee.

Diamandis, Peter H., and Steven Kotler. 2020. The Future Is Faster Than You Think: How Converging Technologies Are Transforming Business, Industries, and Our Lives. Simon and Schuster.

Teixeira, Renata Roland, Miguel Mauricio Díaz, Tatiane Vanessa da Silva Santos, Jean Tofoles Martins Bernardes, Leonardo Gomes Peixoto, Olga Lucia Bocanegra, Morun Bernardino Neto, and Foued Salmen Espindola. 2015. "Chronic Stress Induces a Hyporeactivity of the Autonomic Nervous System in Response to Acute Mental Stressor and Impairs Cognitive Performance in Business Executives." *PloS One* 10 (3): e0119025. Teixeira2015-kq

https://www.shrm.org/resourcesandtools/hr-topics/employee-relations/pages/employee-burnout.aspx; Dana Wilkie, January 31 2017.

Raghupathi, Wullianallur, and Viju Raghupathi. 2018. "An Empirical Study of Chronic Diseases in the United States: A Visual Analytics Approach to Public Health." *International Journal of Environmental Research and Public Health* 15 (3): 431.

Chapter 1: The Autonomic Nervous System: You Self-Regulatory Super-Power

https://www.cdc.gov/chronicdisease/resources/infographic/chronic-diseases.htm

McEwen, Bruce S., and Peter J. Gianaros. 2011. "Stress- and Allostasis-Induced Brain Plasticity." *Annual Review of Medicine* 62: 431–45.

https://www.medicalnewstoday.com/articles/327450#summary What is the Autonomic Nervous System. Medically reviewed by Nancy Hammond, MD on January 10, 2020 — Written by Aaron Kandola

Bill Blessing and Ian Gibbins (2008) Autonomic nervous system. Scholarpedia, 3(7):2787.

Bill Blessing and Ian Gibbins (2008) <a href="http://www.scholarpedia.org/article/Autonomic_nervous_system">Autonomic nervous system</a>. <a href="http://www.scholarpedia.org/">Scholarpedia</a>, 3(7):2787.

Picard, Martin, Bruce S. McEwen, Elissa S. Epel, and Carmen Sandi. 2018. "An Energetic View of Stress: Focus on Mitochondria." *Frontiers in Neuroendocrinology* 49 (April): 72–85.

Teixeira, Renata Roland, Miguel Mauricio Díaz, Tatiane Vanessa da Silva Santos, Jean Tofoles Martins Bernardes, Leonardo Gomes Peixoto, Olga Lucia Bocanegra, Morun Bernardino Neto, and Foued Salmen Espindola. 2015. "Chronic Stress Induces a Hyporeactivity of the Autonomic Nervous System in Response to Acute Mental Stressor and Impairs Cognitive Performance in Business Executives." *PloS One* 10 (3): e0119025. Teixeira2015-kq

Botek, M., A. J. McKune, J. Krejci, P. Stejskal, and A. Gaba. 2014. "Change in Performance in Response to Training Load Adjustment Based on Autonomic Activity." *International Journal of Sports Medicine* 35 (6): 482–88. Botek, M., A. J. McKune, J. Krejci, P. Stejskal, and A. Gaba. 2014. "Change in Performance in Response to Training Load Adjustment Based on Autonomic Activity." *International Journal of Sports Medicine* 35 (6): 482–88.

Caterini, R., G. Delhomme, A. Dittmar, S. Economides, and E. Vernet-Maury. 1993. "A Model of Sporting Performance Constructed from Autonomic Nervous System Responses." *European Journal of Applied Physiology and Occupational Physiology* 67 (3): 250–55.

Strigo, Irina A., and Arthur D. Bud Craig. 2016. "Interoception, Homeostatic Emotions and Sympathovagal Balance." Philosophical

Transactions of the Royal Society of London. Series B, Biological Sciences 371 (1708). https://doi.org/10.1098/rstb.2016.0010.

Thayer, Julian F., and Jos F. Brosschot. 2005. "Psychosomatics and Psychopathology: Looking up and down from the Brain." *Psychoneuroendocrinology* 30 (10): 1050–58.

Thayer, Julian F., Shelby S. Yamamoto, and Jos F. Brosschot. 2010. "The Relationship of Autonomic Imbalance, Heart Rate Variability and Cardiovascular Disease Risk Factors." *International Journal of Cardiology* 141 (2): 122–31.

Engeser, S. E. 2012. "Advances in Flow Research." Edited by Stefan Engeser 231. https://doi.org/10.1007/978-1-4614-2359-1.

Carnethon, Mercedes R., David R. Jacobs Jr, Stephen Sidney, Kiang Liu, and CARDIA study. 2003. "Influence of Autonomic Nervous System Dysfunction on the Development of Type 2 Diabetes: The CARDIA Study." *Diabetes Care* 26 (11): 3035–41.

Noel Bairey Merz, C., Omeed Elboudwarej, and Puja Mehta. 2015. "The Autonomic Nervous System and Cardiovascular Health and Disease." *JACC: Heart Failure* 3 (5): 383–85.

Seals, Douglas R., and Christopher Bell. 2004. "Chronic Sympathetic Activation: Consequence and Cause of Age-Associated Obesity?" *Diabetes* 53 (2): 276–84.

Kenney, M. J., and C. K. Ganta. 2014. "Autonomic Nervous System and Immune System Interactions." *Comprehensive Physiology* 4 (3): 1177–1200.

Koopman, Frieda A., Susanne P. Stoof, Rainer H. Straub, Marjolein A. Van Maanen, Margriet J. Vervoordeldonk, and Paul P. Tak. 2011. "Restoring the Balance of the Autonomic Nervous System as an Innovative Approach to the Treatment of Rheumatoid Arthritis." *Molecular Medicine* 17 (9-10): 937–48.

Brain Wave Frequencies and dysregulation

D. Corydon Hammond (2011) What is Neurofeedback: An Update, Journal of Neurotherapy: Investigations in Neuromodulation, Neurofeedback and Applied Neuroscience, 15:4, 305-336, DOI: 10.1080/10874208.2011.623090

https://brainworksneurotherapy.com/what-are-brainwaves

Circadian Science

Hirshkowitz, Max, Kaitlyn Whiton, Steven M. Albert, Cathy Alessi, Oliviero Bruni, Lydia DonCarlos, Nancy Hazen, et al. 2015. "National Sleep

Foundation's Sleep Time Duration Recommendations: Methodology and Results Summary." *Sleep Health* 1 (1): 40–43.

Walker, Matthew. 2017. *Why We Sleep: Unlocking the Power of Sleep and Dreams*. Simon and Schuster.

Chris Winter, W. 2017. *The Sleep Solution: Why Your Sleep Is Broken and How to Fix It*. Penguin.

Panda, Satchidananda. 2019. "The Arrival of Circadian Medicine." *Nature Reviews. Endocrinology* 15 (2): 67–69.

Panda, Satchin. 2020. *The Circadian Code: Lose Weight, Supercharge Your Energy, and Transform Your Health from Morning to Midnight*. Potter/TenSpeed/Harmony/Rodale.

Manoogian, Emily N. C., Amandine Chaix, and Satchidananda Panda. 2019. "When to Eat: The Importance of Eating Patterns in Health and Disease." *Journal of Biological Rhythms*, 0748730419892105.

McEwen, Bruce S., and Ilia N. Karatsoreos. 2015. "Sleep Deprivation and Circadian Disruption: Stress, Allostasis, and Allostatic Load." *Sleep Medicine Clinics* 10 (1): 1–10.

Mazzotti, Diego Robles, Camila Guindalini, Walter André Dos Santos Moraes, Monica Levy Andersen, Maysa Seabra Cendoroglo, Luiz Roberto Ramos, and Sergio Tufik. 2014. "Human Longevity Is Associated with Regular Sleep Patterns, Maintenance of Slow Wave Sleep, and Favorable Lipid Profile." *Frontiers in Aging Neuroscience* 6 (June): 134.

Heart Rate Variability

Berntson, G. G., Bigger, J. T., Eckberg, D. L., Grossman, P., Kaufmann, P. G., Malik, M., et al. (1997). Heart rate variability: Origins, methods, and interpretive caveats. *Psychophysiology, 34*(6), 623-648.

Grossarth-Maticek, R., and H. J. Eysenck. 1995. "Self-Regulation and Mortality from Cancer, Coronary Heart Disease, and Other Causes: A Prospective Study." *Personality and Individual Differences* 19 (6): 781–95.

Thayer, J. F., Ahs, F., Fredrikson, M., Sollers, J. J., & Wager, T. D. (2012). A meta-analysis of heart rate variability and neuroimaging studies: Implications for heart rate variability as a marker of stress and health. *Neuroscience and Biobehavioral Reviews, 36*, 747-756.

Thayer, J. F., Yamamoto, S. S., & Brosschot, J. F. (2010). The relationship of autonomic imbalance, heart rate variability and cardiovascular disease risk factors. *Int J Cardiol, 141*(2), 122-131.

https://videoclub.me/mobile/video/7k3mdAPmIdo

Aeschbacher, Stefanie, Tobias Schoen, Laura Dörig, Rahel Kreuzmann, Charlotte Neuhauser, Arno Schmidt-Trucksäss, Nicole M. Probst-Hensch, Martin Risch, Lorenz Risch, and David Conen. 2017. "Heart Rate, Heart Rate Variability and Inflammatory Biomarkers among Young and Healthy Adults." *Annals of Medicine* 49 (1): 32–41.

Almeida-Santos, Marcos Antonio, Jose Augusto Barreto-Filho, Joselina Luzia Menezes Oliveira, Francisco Prado Reis, Cristiane Costa da Cunha Oliveira, and Antonio Carlos Sobral Sousa. 2016. "Aging, Heart Rate Variability and Patterns of Autonomic Regulation of the Heart." *Archives of Gerontology and Geriatrics* 63 (March): 1–8.

Kemp, Andrew H., Daniel S. Quintana, Kim L. Felmingham, Slade Matthews, and Herbert F. Jelinek. 2012. "Depression, Comorbid Anxiety Disorders, and Heart Rate Variability in Physically Healthy, Unmedicated Patients: Implications for Cardiovascular Risk." *PloS One* 7 (2): e30777.

Maheshwari, Ankit, Faye L. Norby, Elsayed Z. Soliman, Selcuk Adabag, Eric A. Whitsel, Alvaro Alonso, and Lin Y. Chen. 2016. "Low Heart Rate Variability in a 2-Minute Electrocardiogram Recording Is Associated with an Increased Risk of Sudden Cardiac Death in the General Population: The Atherosclerosis Risk in Communities Study." *PloS One* 11 (8): e0161648.

Neurobiology

Wikipedia contributors. (2020, March 16). Neurotransmitter. In *Wikipedia, The Free Encyclopedia*. Retrieved 11:10, March 27, 2020, from https://en.wikipedia.org/w/index.php?title=Neurotransmitter&oldid=945772563

https://www.medicalnewstoday.com/articles/326649 Oct 11, 2019 Jennifer Berry

https://www.verywellmind.com/what-is-a-neurotransmitter-2795394 Dec 7, 2019 Kendra Cherry

Briguglio, M., Dell'Osso, B., Panzica, G., Malgaroli, A., Banfi, G., Zanaboni Dina, C., Galentino, R., & Porta, M. (2018). Dietary Neurotransmitters: A Narrative Review on Current Knowledge. *Nutrients, 10*(5), 591. https://doi.org/10.3390/nu10050591

https://snowbrains.com/the-brain-science-behind-flow-states/ August 2, 2019 Martin Kuprianowicz

Chapter 2: 8 Biohacking Habits to Optimize Your Health

Habit 1: Train Your Brain Through Neurofeedback

Larsen, Stephen, and Leslie Sherlin. 2013. "Neurofeedback: An Emerging Technology for Treating Central Nervous System Dysregulation." *The Psychiatric Clinics of North America* 36 (1): 163–68.

Steiner, Naomi J., Elizabeth C. Frenette, Kirsten M. Rene, Robert T. Brennan, and Ellen C. Perrin. 2014. "In-School Neurofeedback Training for ADHD: Sustained Improvements from a Randomized Control Trial." *Pediatrics* 133 (3): 483–92.

Munivenkatappa, Ashok, Jamuna Rajeswaran, Bhagavatula Indira Devi, Niranjana Bennet, and Neeraj Upadhyay. 2014. "EEG Neurofeedback Therapy: Can It Attenuate Brain Changes in TBI?" *NeuroRehabilitation* 35 (3): 481–84.

Gruzelier, John, Tobias Egner, and David Vernon. 2006. "Validating the Efficacy of Neurofeedback for Optimising Performance." *Progress in Brain Research* 159: 421–31.

Gruzelier, John H. 2014. "EEG-Neurofeedback for Optimising Performance. I: A Review of Cognitive and Affective Outcome in Healthy Participants." *Neuroscience and Biobehavioral Reviews* 44 (July): 124–41.

Hatfield, B., A. Haufler, and J. Contreras-Vidal. 2009. "Brain Processes and Neurofeedback for Performance Enhancement of Precision Motor Behavior." In *Foundations of Augmented Cognition. Neuroergonomics and Operational Neuroscience*, 810–17. Springer Berlin Heidelberg.

D. Corydon Hammond (2011) What is Neurofeedback: An Update, Journal of Neurotherapy: Investigations in Neuromodulation, Neurofeedback and Applied Neuroscience, 15:4, 305-336, DOI: 10.1080/10874208.2011.623090

https://www.cwilsonmeloncelli.com/the-5-brain-waves-and-it s-connection-with-flow-state/

Habit 2: Transform Your Performance Through Heart Rate Variability

Lehrer, Paul M., and Richard Gevirtz. 2014. "Heart Rate Variability Biofeedback: How and Why Does It Work?" *Frontiers in Psychology* 5 (July): 756.

Mather, Mara, and Julian Thayer. 2018. "How Heart Rate Variability Affects Emotion Regulation Brain Networks." *Current Opinion in Behavioral Sciences* 19 (February): 98–104.

Aeschbacher, Stefanie, Matthias Bossard, Tobias Schoen, Delia Schmidlin, Christoph Muff, Anna Maseli, Jörg D. Leuppi, et al. 2016. "Heart Rate Variability and Sleep-Related Breathing Disorders in the General Population." *The American Journal of Cardiology* 118 (6): 912–17.

Sakaki, Michiko, Hyun Joo Yoo, Lin Nga, Tae-Ho Lee, Julian F. Thayer, and Mara Mather. 2016. "Heart Rate Variability Is Associated with Amygdala Functional Connectivity with MPFC across Younger and Older Adults." *NeuroImage* 139 (October): 44–52.

Wei, Luqing, Hong Chen, and Guo-Rong Wu. 2018. "Structural Covariance of the Prefrontal-Amygdala Pathways Associated with Heart Rate Variability." *Frontiers in Human Neuroscience* 12 (January): 2.

Bassett, Darryl. 2016. "A Literature Review of Heart Rate Variability in Depressive and Bipolar Disorders." *The Australian and New Zealand Journal of Psychiatry* 50 (6): 511–19.

Britton, A., A. Singh-Manoux, K. Hnatkova, M. Malik, M. G. Marmot, and M. Shipley. 2008. "The Association between Heart Rate Variability and Cognitive Impairment in Middle-Aged Men and Women." *Neuroepidemiology* 31 (2): 115–21.

Thayer, Julian F., Shelby S. Yamamoto, and Jos F. Brosschot. 2010. "The Relationship of Autonomic Imbalance, Heart Rate Variability and Cardiovascular Disease Risk Factors." *International Journal of Cardiology* 141 (2): 122–31.

Jiménez Morgan, Sergio, and José Arturo Molina Mora. 2017. "Effect of Heart Rate Variability Biofeedback on Sport Performance, a Systematic Review." *Applied Psychophysiology and Biofeedback* 42 (3): 235–45.

Fatisson, Julien, Victor Oswald, and François Lalonde. 2016. "Influence Diagram of Physiological and Environmental Factors Affecting Heart Rate Variability: An Extended Literature Overview." *Heart International* 11 (1): e32–40.

Luque-Casado, Antonio, Mikel Zabala, Esther Morales, Manuel Mateo-March, and Daniel Sanabria. 2013. "Cognitive Performance and Heart Rate Variability: The Influence of Fitness Level." *PloS One* 8 (2): e56935.

Sutarto, Auditya Purwandini, Muhammad Nubli Abdul Wahab, and Nora Mat Zin. 2010. "Heart Rate Variability (HRV) Biofeedback: A New Training Approach for Operator's Performance Enhancement." *Journal of Industrial Engineering and Management* 3 (1): 176–98

Paul, Maman, and Kanupriya Garg. 2012. "The Effect of Heart Rate Variability Biofeedback on Performance Psychology of Basketball Players." *Applied Psychophysiology and Biofeedback* 37 (2): 131–44.

Thurber, Myron R., Eugenia Bodenhamer-Davis, Mark Johnson, Kris Chesky, and Cynthia K. Chandler. 2010. "Effects of Heart Rate Variability Coherence Biofeedback Training and Emotional Management Techniques to Decrease Music Performance Anxiety." *Biofeedback and Self-Regulation* 38 (1): 28–40.

Kim, Sonya, Vance Zemon, Marie M. Cavallo, Joseph F. Rath, Rollin McCraty, and Frederick W. Foley. 2013. "Heart Rate Variability Biofeedback, Executive Functioning and Chronic Brain Injury." *Brain Injury: [BI]* 27 (2): 209–22.

Aeschbacher, Stefanie, Matthias Bossard, Francisco Javier Ruperti Repilado, Nathalie Good, Tobias Schoen, Matylda Zimny, Nicole M. Probst-Hensch, et al. 2016. "Healthy Lifestyle and Heart Rate Variability in Young Adults." *European Journal of Preventive Cardiology* 23 (10): 1037–44.

Boehm, Julia K., and Laura D. Kubzansky. 2012. "The Heart's Content: The Association between Positive Psychological Well-Being and Cardiovascular Health." *Psychological Bulletin* 138 (4): 655–91.

Dietrich, Denise Felber, Ursula Ackermann-Liebrich, Christian Schindler, Jean-Claude Barthélémy, Otto Brändli, Diane R. Gold, Bruno Knöpfli, et al. 2008. "Effect of Physical Activity on Heart Rate Variability in Normal Weight, Overweight and Obese Subjects: Results from the SAPALDIA Study." *European Journal of Applied Physiology* 104 (3): 557–65.

Geisler, Fay C. M., Thomas Kubiak, Kerstin Siewert, and Hannelore Weber. 2013. "Cardiac Vagal Tone Is Associated with Social Engagement and Self-Regulation." *Biological Psychology* 93 (2): 279–86.

Gladwell, Valerie F., Pekka Kuoppa, Mika P. Tarvainen, and Mike Rogerson. 2016. "A Lunchtime Walk in Nature Enhances Restoration of Autonomic Control during Night-Time Sleep: Results from a Preliminary Study." *International Journal of Environmental Research and Public Health* 13 (3). https://doi.org/10.3390/ijerph13030280.

Nijjar, Prabhjot Singh, Venkata Krishna Puppala, Oana Dickinson, Sue Duval, Daniel Duprez, Mary J. Kreitzer, and David G. Benditt. 2014. "Modulation of the Autonomic Nervous System Assessed through Heart Rate Variability by a Mindfulness Based Stress Reduction Program." *International Journal of Cardiology* 177 (2): 557–59.

Tharion, Elizabeth, Prasanna Samuel, R. Rajalakshmi, G. Gnanasenthil, and Rajam Krishna Subramanian. 2012. "Influence of Deep Breathing Exercise on Spontaneous Respiratory Rate and Heart Rate Variability: A Randomised Controlled Trial in Healthy Subjects." *Indian Journal of Physiology and Pharmacology* 56 (1): 80–87.

Zulfiqar, Usman, Donald A. Jurivich, Weihua Gao, and Donald H. Singer. 2010. "Relation of High Heart Rate Variability to Healthy Longevity." *The American Journal of Cardiology* 105 (8): 1181–85.

Quintana, Daniel S., Adam J. Guastella, Tim Outhred, Ian B. Hickie, and Andrew H. Kemp. 2012. "Heart Rate Variability Is Associated with Emotion Recognition: Direct Evidence for a Relationship between the Autonomic Nervous System and Social Cognition." *International Journal of Psychophysiology: Official Journal of the International Organization of Psychophysiology* 86 (2): 168–72.

Thayer, Julian F., Anita L. Hansen, Evelyn Saus-Rose, and Bjorn Helge Johnsen. 2009. "Heart Rate Variability, Prefrontal Neural Function, and Cognitive Performance: The Neurovisceral Integration Perspective on Self-Regulation, Adaptation, and Health." *Annals of Behavioral Medicine: A Publication of the Society of Behavioral Medicine* 37 (2): 141–53.

Habit 3: The Science Behind Meditation

Garrison, Kathleen A., Thomas A. Zeffiro, Dustin Scheinost, R. Todd Constable, and Judson A. Brewer. 2015. "Meditation Leads to Reduced Default Mode Network Activity beyond an Active Task." *Cognitive, Affective & Behavioral Neuroscience* 15 (3): 712–20.

Hölzel, Britta K., James Carmody, Mark Vangel, Christina Congleton, Sita M. Yerramsetti, Tim Gard, and Sara W. Lazar. 2011. "Mindfulness Practice Leads to Increases in Regional Brain Gray Matter Density." *Psychiatry Research* 191 (1): 36–43.

Luders, Eileen, Nicolas Cherbuin, and Florian Kurth. 2014. "Forever Young(er): Potential Age-Defying Effects of Long-Term Meditation on Gray Matter Atrophy." *Frontiers in Psychology* 5: 1551.

Praissman, S. 2008. "Mindfulness–based Stress Reduction: A Literature Review and Clinician's Guide." *Journal of the American Academy of Nurse Practitioners*. https://onlinelibrary.wiley.com/doi/abs/10.111 1/j.1745-7599.2008.00306.

Chiesa, Alberto, Raffaella Calati, and Alessandro Serretti. 2011. "Does Mindfulness Training Improve Cognitive Abilities? A Systematic Review of Neuropsychological Findings." *Clinical Psychology Review* 31 (3): 449–64.

Goyal, Madhav, Sonal Singh, Erica M. S. Sibinga, Neda F. Gould, Anastasia Rowland-Seymour, Ritu Sharma, Zackary Berger, et al. 2014. "Meditation Programs for Psychological Stress and Well-Being: A Systematic Review and Meta-Analysis." *JAMA Internal Medicine* 174 (3): 357–68.

Epel, Elissa, Jennifer Daubenmier, Judith T. Moskowitz, Susan Folkman, and Elizabeth Blackburn. 2009. "Can Meditation Slow Rate of Cellular Aging? Cognitive Stress, Mindfulness, and Telomeres." *Annals of the New York Academy of Sciences* 1172: 34.

Brown, Richard P., and Patricia L. Gerbarg. 2009. "Yoga Breathing, Meditation, and Longevity." *Annals of the New York Academy of Sciences* 1172 (August): 54–62.

Shearer, Annie, Melissa Hunt, Mifta Chowdhury, and Lorena Nicol. 2016. "Effects of a Brief Mindfulness Meditation Intervention on Student Stress and Heart Rate Variability." *International Journal of Stress Management* 23 (2): 232.

Ching, Ho-Hoi, Malcolm Koo, Tsung-Huang Tsai, and Chiu-Yuan Chen. 2015. "Effects of a Mindfulness Meditation Course on Learning and Cognitive Performance among University Students in Taiwan." *Evidence-Based Complementary and Alternative Medicine: eCAM* 2015 (November): 254358.

Chan, John S. Y., Kanfeng Deng, Jiamin Wu, and Jin H. Yan. 2019. "Effects of Meditation and Mind—Body Exercises on Older Adults' Cognitive Performance: A Meta-Analysis." *The Gerontologist* 59 (6): e782–90.

Kaufman, Keith A., Carol R. Glass, and Diane B. Arnkoff. 2009. "Evaluation of Mindful Sport Performance Enhancement (MSPE): A New Approach to Promote Flow in Athletes." *Journal of Clinical Sport Psychology* 3 (4): 334–56.

Habit 4: Move to Change Your Brain and Build Your Engine for Performance

Lauenroth, Andreas, Anestis E. Ioannidis, and Birgit Teichmann. 2016. "Influence of Combined Physical and Cognitive Training on Cognition: A Systematic Review." *BMC Geriatrics* 16 (July): 141.

Ratey, John J. 2008. *Spark: The Revolutionary New Science of Exercise and the Brain*. Little, Brown.

Luque-Casado, Antonio, Pandelis Perakakis, Charles H. Hillman, Shih-Chun Kao, Francesc Llorens, Pedro Guerra, and Daniel Sanabria. 2016. "Differences in Sustained Attention Capacity as a Function of Aerobic Fitness." *Medicine and Science in Sports and Exercise* 48 (5): 887–95.

Mechling, Heinz, and Yael Netz. 2009. "Aging and Inactivity—capitalizing on the Protective Effect of Planned Physical Activity in Old Age." *European Review of Aging and Physical Activity: Official Journal of the European Group for Research into Elderly and Physical Activity* 6 (2): 89.

Folkins, C. H., and W. E. Sime. 1981. "Physical Fitness Training and Mental Health." *The American Psychologist* 36 (4): 373–89.

Landi, Francesco, Angela M. Abbatecola, Mauro Provinciali, Andrea Corsonello, Silvia Bustacchini, Luca Manigrasso, Antonio Cherubini, Roberto Bernabei, and Fabrizia Lattanzio. 2010. "Moving against Frailty: Does Physical Activity Matter?" *Biogerontology* 11 (5): 537–45.

Williams, Kristine N., and Susan Kemper. 2010. "Interventions to Reduce Cognitive Decline in Aging." *Journal of Psychosocial Nursing and Mental Health Services* 48 (5): 42–51.

Kumar, Namrita, Lewis A. Wheaton, Teresa K. Snow, and Melinda Millard-Stafford. 2015. "Exercise and Caffeine Improve Sustained Attention Following Fatigue Independent of Fitness Status." *Fatigue: Biomedicine, Health & Behavior* 3 (2): 104–21.

Chaddock, Laura, Charles H. Hillman, Matthew B. Pontifex, Christopher R. Johnson, Lauren B. Raine, and Arthur F. Kramer. 2012. "Childhood Aerobic Fitness Predicts Cognitive Performance One Year Later." *Journal of Sports Sciences* 30 (5): 421–30.

Lovelace, Kathi J., Charles C. Manz, and José C. Alves. 2007. "Work Stress and Leadership Development: The Role of Self-Leadership, Shared Leadership, Physical Fitness and Flow in Managing Demands and Increasing Job Control." *Human Resource Management Review* 17 (4): 374–87.

Stanten, Michele, Elson, Lauren E. MD. 2019. "Walking for Health, Why This Simple Activity Could Be Your Best Health Insurance." *Harvard Medical School Special Health Report*: pp 3-6

Habit 5: Fuel Your Body for Elite Performance

https://www.healthline.com/nutrition/
how-to-increase-glutathione#section1

Joseph, James, Greg Cole, Elizabeth Head, and Donald Ingram. 2009. "Nutrition, Brain Aging, and Neurodegeneration." *The Journal of Neuroscience: The Official Journal of the Society for Neuroscience* 29 (41): 12795–801.

Andersen, Catherine J., and Maria Luz Fernandez. 2013. "Dietary Strategies to Reduce Metabolic Syndrome." *Reviews in Endocrine & Metabolic Disorders* 14 (3): 241–54.

Wu, Lingyun, M. Hossein Noyan Ashraf, Marina Facci, Rui Wang, Phyllis G. Paterson, Alison Ferrie, and Bernhard H. J. Juurlink. 2004. "Dietary Approach to Attenuate Oxidative Stress, Hypertension, and Inflammation in the Cardiovascular System." *Proceedings of the National Academy of Sciences of the United States of America* 101 (18): 7094–99.

Blackburn, Elizabeth, and Elissa Epel. 2017. *The Telomere Effect: A Revolutionary Approach to Living Younger, Healthier, Longer.* Hachette UK. 224-241

Tucker, Larry A. 2017. "Caffeine Consumption and Telomere Length in Men and Women of the National Health and Nutrition Examination Survey (NHANES)." *Nutrition & Metabolism* 14 (January): 10.

Boccardi, Virginia, Giuseppe Paolisso, and Patrizia Mecocci. 2016. "Nutrition and Lifestyle in Healthy Aging: The Telomerase Challenge." *Aging* 8 (1): 12–15. Galland, Leo. 2010. "Diet and Inflammation." *Nutrition in Clinical Practice: Official Publication of the American Society for Parenteral and Enteral Nutrition* 25 (6): 634–40.

Stafstrom, Carl E., and Jong M. Rho. 2012. "The Ketogenic Diet as a Treatment Paradigm for Diverse Neurological Disorders." *Frontiers in Pharmacology* 3 (April): 59.

Vetrani, C., G. Costabile, L. Di Marino, and A. A. Rivellese. 2013. "Nutrition and Oxidative Stress: A Systematic Review of Human Studies." *International Journal of Food Sciences and Nutrition* 64 (3): 312–26. Galland, Leo. 2010. "Diet and Inflammation." *Nutrition in Clinical Practice: Official Publication of the American Society for Parenteral and Enteral Nutrition* 25 (6): 634–40.

García-Calzón, Sonia, Guillermo Zalba, Miguel Ruiz-Canela, Nitin Shivappa, James R. Hébert, J. Alfredo

Murray, Andrew J., Nicholas S. Knight, Mark A. Cole, Lowri E. Cochlin, Emma Carter, Kirill Tchabanenko, Tica Pichulik, et al. 2016. "Novel Ketone Diet Enhances Physical and Cognitive Performance." *FASEB Journal: Official Publication of the Federation of American Societies for Experimental Biology* 30 (12): 4021–32.

Scarmeas, Nikolaos. 2013. "Mediterranean Food for Thought?" *Journal of Neurology, Neurosurgery, and Psychiatry* 84 (12): 1297–1297.

Crous-Bou, Marta, Teresa T. Fung, Jennifer Prescott, Bettina Julin, Mengmeng Du, Qi Sun, Kathryn M. Rexrode, Frank B. Hu, and Immaculata

De Vivo. 2014. "Mediterranean Diet and Telomere Length in Nurses' Health Study: Population Based Cohort Study." *BMJ* 349 (December): g6674.

Habit 6: Hydration for Optimal Physical and Cognitive Function

Benton, David, and Hayley A. Young. 2015. "Do Small Differences in Hydration Status Affect Mood and Mental Performance?" *Nutrition Reviews* 73 Suppl 2 (September): 83–96.

Edmonds, Caroline J., and Denise Burford. 2009. "Should Children Drink More Water?: The Effects of Drinking Water on Cognition in Children." *Appetite* 52 (3): 776–79.

https://medium.com/bsxtechnologies/4-ways-dehyd
ration-affects-your-brain-e4042a6cb6b1

https://www.mayoclinic.org/healthy-lifestyle/
nutrition-and-healthy-eating/in-depth/water/art-20044256

Kenefick, Robert W., and Samuel N. Cheuvront. 2012. "Hydration for Recreational Sport and Physical Activity." *Nutrition Reviews* 70 Suppl 2 (November): S137–42.

Kolasa, Kathryn M., Carolyn J. Lackey, and Ann C. Grandjean. 2009. "Hydration and Health Promotion." *Nutrition Today* 44 (5): 190.

Masento, Natalie A., Mark Golightly, David T. Field, Laurie T. Butler, and Carien M. van Reekum. 2014. "Effects of Hydration Status on Cognitive Performance and Mood." *The British Journal of Nutrition* 111 (10): 1841–52.

Merhej, Rita. 2019. "Dehydration and Cognition: An Understated Relation." *International Journal of Health Governance* 24 (1): 19–30.

Popkin, Barry M., Kristen E. D'Anci, and Irwin H. Rosenberg. 2010. "Water, Hydration, and Health." *Nutrition Reviews* 68 (8): 439–58.

Shirreffs, Susan M. 2005. "The Importance of Good Hydration for Work and Exercise Performance." *Nutrition Reviews* 63 (6 Pt 2): S14–21.

Habit 7: Sleep Optimization

Feld, Gordon B., and Susanne Diekelmann. 2015. "Sleep Smart-Optimizing Sleep for Declarative Learning and Memory." *Frontiers in Psychology* 6 (May): 622.

Zlokovic, Berislav V., Rashid Deane, Abhay P. Sagare, Robert D. Bell, and Ethan A. Winkler. 2010. "Low-Density Lipoprotein Receptor-Related

Protein-1: A Serial Clearance Homeostatic Mechanism Controlling Alzheimer's Amyloid β-Peptide Elimination from the Brain." *Journal of Neurochemistry* 115 (5): 1077–89.

Mazzotti, Diego Robles, Camila Guindalini, Walter André Dos Santos Moraes, Monica Levy Andersen, Maysa Seabra Cendoroglo, Luiz Roberto Ramos, and Sergio Tufik. 2014. "Human Longevity Is Associated with Regular Sleep Patterns, Maintenance of Slow Wave Sleep, and Favorable Lipid Profile." *Frontiers in Aging Neuroscience* 6 (June): 134.

McEwen, Bruce S., and Ilia N. Karatsoreos. 2015. "Sleep Deprivation and Circadian Disruption: Stress, Allostasis, and Allostatic Load." *Sleep Medicine Clinics* 10 (1): 1–10.

Simpson, N. S., E. L. Gibbs, and G. O. Matheson. 2017. "Optimizing Sleep to Maximize Performance: Implications and Recommendations for Elite Athletes." *Scandinavian Journal of Medicine & Science in Sports* 27 (3): 266–74.

Takahashi, Masaya. 2012. "Prioritizing Sleep for Healthy Work Schedules." *Journal of Physiological Anthropology* 31 (March): 6.

Zepelin, Harold, and Allan Rechtschaffen. 1974. "Mammalian Sleep, Longevity, and Energy Metabolism; Pp. 447—470." *Brain, Behavior and Evolution* 10 (6): 447–70.

Habit 8: When You Eat Matters More than What You Eat—Performance Nutrition Simplified

Collier, Roger. 2013. "Intermittent Fasting: The Science of Going without." *CMAJ: Canadian Medical Association Journal = Journal de l'Association Medicale Canadienne* 185 (9): E363–64.

Golbidi, Saeid, Andreas Daiber, Bato Korac, Huige Li, M. Faadiel Essop, and Ismail Laher. 2017. "Health Benefits of Fasting and Caloric Restriction." *Current Diabetes Reports* 17 (12): 123.

Hutchison, Amy T., Prashant Regmi, Emily N. C. Manoogian, Jason G. Fleischer, Gary A. Wittert, Satchidananda Panda, and Leonie K. Heilbronn. 2019. "Time–Restricted Feeding Improves Glucose Tolerance in Men at Risk for Type 2 Diabetes: A Randomized Crossover Trial." *Obesity* 26 (April): 759.

Longo, Valter D., and Satchidananda Panda. 2016. "Fasting, Circadian Rhythms, and Time-Restricted Feeding in Healthy Lifespan." *Cell Metabolism* 23 (6): 1048–59.

Manoogian, Emily N. C., Amandine Chaix, and Satchidananda Panda. 2019. "When to Eat: The Importance of Eating Patterns in Health and Disease." *Journal of Biological Rhythms*, 0748730419892105.

Mattson, Mark P., Valter D. Longo, and Michelle Harvie. 2017. "Impact of Intermittent Fasting on Health and Disease Processes." *Ageing Research Reviews* 39 (October): 46–58.

Tinsley, Grant M., and Paul M. La Bounty. 2015. "Effects of Intermittent Fasting on Body Composition and Clinical Health Markers in Humans." *Nutrition Reviews* 73 (10): 661–74.

Van Praag, Henriette, Monika Fleshner, Michael W. Schwartz, and Mark P. Mattson. 2014. "Exercise, Energy Intake, Glucose Homeostasis, and the Brain." *Journal of Neuroscience* 34 (46): 15139–49.

Wilkinson, Michael J., Emily N. C. Manoogian, Adena Zadourian, Hannah Lo, Savannah Fakhouri, Azarin Shoghi, Xinran Wang, et al. 2020. "Ten-Hour Time-Restricted Eating Reduces Weight, Blood Pressure, and Atherogenic Lipids in Patients with Metabolic Syndrome." *Cell Metabolism* 31 (1): 92–104.e5.

Chapter 3: Psychology Pillars for Elite Performance

Development of Mindset

Dweck, Carol. 2015. "Carol Dweck Revisits the Growth Mindset." *Education Week* 35 (5): 20–24.

"What Having a 'growth Mindset' Actually Means." *Harvard Business Review* 13: 213–26. 2016

Hallett, Matthew G., and Bobby Hoffman. 2014. "Performing under Pressure: Cultivating the Peak Performance Mindset for Workplace Excellence." *Consulting Psychology Journal: Practice and Research* 66 (3): 212–30.

Hochanadel, Aaron, and Dora Finamore. 2015. "Fixed And Growth Mindset In Education And How Grit Helps Students Persist In The Face Of Adversity." *Journal of International Education Research (JIER)* 11 (1): 47–50.

Visser, Coert F. 2013. "Professional Helpers' Growth Mindset, Work Engagement and Self-Reported Performance." *Wagner, K. , Brinkmann, J. , March, S. , Hinterstoißer, P. , Warnecke, S. , Schüler, M. and Paulsen, HM (2018) Impact of Daily Grazing Time on Dairy Cow Welfare-Results of the Welfare Quality® Protocol. Animals* 8: 1–11.

Dweck, Carol S. 2008. *Mindset: The New Psychology of Success.* Ballantine Books.

"Mindsets: Developing Talent through a Growth Mindset." *Olympic Coach* 21 (1): 4–7. 2009

Locus of Control

Wikipedia contributors. (2020, April 15). Locus of control. In *Wikipedia, The Free Encyclopedia.* Retrieved 10:55, May 15, 2020, from https://en.wikipedia.org/w/index. php?title=Locus_of_control&oldid=951061021

Rotter, Julian B (1966). "Generalized expectancies for internal versus external control of reinforcement". Psychological Monographs: General and Applied. **80**: 1–28. doi:10.1037/h0092976

Self-Efficacy - Belief

Bandura, Albert. 2010. "Self-Efficacy." *The Corsini Encyclopedia of Psychology,* 1–3.

Seligman, Martin E. P., and Mihaly Csikszentmihalyi. 2014. "Positive Psychology: An Introduction." In *Flow and the Foundations of Positive Psychology: The Collected Works of Mihaly Csikszentmihalyi,* edited by Mihaly Csikszentmihalyi, 279–98. Dordrecht: Springer Netherlands.

Bray, Steven R., Isabel Balaguer, and Joan L. Duda. 2004. "The Relationship of Task Self-Efficacy and Role Efficacy Beliefs to Role Performance in Spanish Youth Soccer." *Journal of Sports Sciences* 22 (5): 429–37.

Cohn, Patrick J. 1991. "An Exploratory Study on Peak Performance in Golf." *Sport Psychologist* 5 (1): 1–14.

Fitzsimmons, P. A., D. M. Landers, J. R. Thomas, and H. van der Mars. 1991. "Does Self-Efficacy Predict Performance in Experienced Weightlifters?" *Research Quarterly for Exercise and Sport* 62 (4): 424–31.

Martin, Jeffrey J., and Diane L. Gill. 1991. "The Relationships Among Competitive Orientation, Sport-Confidence, Self-Efficacy, Anxiety, and Performance." *Journal of Sport and Exercise Psychology* 13 (2): 149–59.

Rotter, Julian. 2004. "Locus of Control." *Cognitive Approach Wrap Up Begin Emotions and Personality. Lecture Notes Psych A* 305. http://ubc-emotionlab.ca/wp-content/uploads/2013/08/ Lecture-20-Cognition-wrap-up-Begin-Emotions.pdf.

Gratitude

Chaudhary, Heera, Sheetal Chaudhary, and Others. 2014. "Positive Emotions, Resilience, Gratitude and Forgiveness: Rrole of Positive Psychology in 21st Century." *Indian Journal of Positive Psychology* 5 (4): 528.

Chen, Lung Hung, Chia-Huei Wu, and Jen-Ho Chang. 2017. "Gratitude and Athletes' Life Satisfaction: The Moderating Role of Mindfulness." *Journal of Happiness Studies* 18 (4): 1147–59.

Cheng, Sheung-Tak, Pui Ki Tsui, and John H. M. Lam. 2015. "Improving Mental Health in Health Care Practitioners: Randomized Controlled Trial of a Gratitude Intervention." *Journal of Consulting and Clinical Psychology* 83 (1): 177–86.

Jans-Beken, Lilian, Nele Jacobs, Mayke Janssens, Sanne Peeters, Jennifer Reijnders, Lilian Lechner, and Johan Lataster. 2019. "Gratitude and Health: An Updated Review." The Journal of Positive Psychology, August, 1–40.

Kini, Prathik, Joel Wong, Sydney McInnis, Nicole Gabana, and Joshua W. Brown. 2016. "The Effects of Gratitude Expression on Neural Activity." *NeuroImage* 128 (March): 1–10.

Southwell, Sharon, and Emma Gould. 2017. "A Randomised Wait List-Controlled Pre–post–follow-up Trial of a Gratitude Diary with a Distressed Sample." *The Journal of Positive Psychology* 12 (6): 579–93.

Grit

Perkins-Gough, Deborah. 2013. "The Significance of Grit: A Conversation with Angela Lee Duckworth." Educational Leadership: Journal of the Department of Supervision and Curriculum Development, N.E.A 71 (1): 14–20.

Duckworth, Angela, and Angela Duckworth. 2016. *Grit: The Power of Passion and Perseverance.* Vol. 234. Scribner New York, NY. Pp 3-10

Duckworth, Angela Lee, and Patrick D. Quinn. 2009. "Development and Validation of the Short Grit Scale (Grit–S)." *Journal of Personality Assessment* 91 (2): 166–74.

Jachimowicz, Jon M., Andreas Wihler, Erica R. Bailey, and Adam D. Galinsky. 2018a. "Why Grit Requires Perseverance and Passion to Positively Predict Performance." *Proceedings of the National Academy of Sciences of the United States of America* 115 (40): 9980–85.

Chapter 4: Implementing Elite Performance Psychology

Intrinsic Motivation

Di Domenico, Stefano I., and Richard M. Ryan. 2017. "The Emerging Neuroscience of Intrinsic Motivation: A New Frontier in Self-Determination Research." *Frontiers in Human Neuroscience* 11 (March): 145.

Abuhamdeh, Sami, and Mihaly Csikszentmihalyi. 2012. "Attentional Involvement and Intrinsic Motivation." *Motivation and Emotion* 36 (3): 257–67.

Keller, Johannes, and Herbert Bless. 2008. "Flow and Regulatory Compatibility: An Experimental Approach to the Flow Model of Intrinsic Motivation." *Personality & Social Psychology Bulletin* 34 (2): 196–209.

Hennessey, B., S. Moran, and B. Altringer. 2015. "Extrinsic and Intrinsic Motivation." In *Wiley Encyclopedia of Management*, edited by Cary L. Cooper, 88:1–4. Chichester, UK: John Wiley & Sons, Ltd.

Oudeyer, Pierre-Yves, Frederic Kaplan, and Others. 2008. "How Can We Define Intrinsic Motivation." In *Proc. of the 8th Conf. on Epigenetic Robotics,* 5:29–31. academia.edu.

Schwartz, Seth J., and Alan S. Waterman. 2006. "Changing Interests: A Longitudinal Study of Intrinsic Motivation for Personally Salient Activities." *Journal of Research in Personality* 40 (6): 1119–36.

Seifert, T., and C. Hedderson. 2010. "Intrinsic Motivation and Flow in Skateboarding: An Ethnographic Study." *Journal of Happiness Studies* 11 (3): 277–92.

Stavrou, Nektarios A. 2008. "Intrinsic Motivation, Extrinsic Motivation and Amotivation: Examining Self-Determination Theory from Flow Theory Perspective." *New Developments in the Psychology of Motivation,* 1–24.

Deci, E. L., R. Koestner, and R. M. Ryan. 1999. "A Meta-Analytic Review of Experiments Examining the Effects of Extrinsic Rewards on Intrinsic Motivation." *Psychological Bulletin* 125 (6): 627–68; discussion 692–700.

Pink, Daniel H. 2011. *Drive: The Surprising Truth About What Motivates Us.* Penguin.

Cultivating Confidence and Belief

The Confidence Gap: A Guide to Overcoming Fear and Self-Doubt. Shambhala Publications. 2011

Powers, Mark B., Maarten B. Zum Vorde Sive Vording, and Paul
M. G. Emmelkamp. 2009. "Acceptance and Commitment Therapy:
A Meta-Analytic Review." *Psychotherapy and Psychosomatics* 78 (2): 73–80.

Core Values

https://www.indeed.com/career-advice/career-development/core-values;
April 2, 2020

https://www.brighthr.com/articles/culture-and-performance/core-values/

https://www.brighthr.com/articles/culture-and-performance/core-values/
how-business-core-values-benefit-employees

Ferguson, Jeffery, and John Milliman. 2008. "Creating Effective Core
Organizational Values: A Spiritual Leadership Approach." *International
Journal of Public Administration* 31 (4): 439–59.

Jin, K. G., and R. G. Drozdenko. 2010. "Relationships among Perceived
Organizational Core Values, Corporate Social Responsibility, Ethics, and
Organizational Performance Outcomes: An Empirical Study of …." *Journal
of Business Ethics: JBE.*

Oh, Jihye, Daeyeon Cho, and Lim Doo Hun. 2018. "Authentic Leadership
and Work Engagement: The Mediating Effect of Practicing Core Values."
Leadership & Organization Development Journal 39 (2): 276–90.

Goal Setting For Performance

Bar-Eli, M., G. Tenenbaum, J. S. Pie, Y. Btesh, and A. Almog. 1997. "Effect
of Goal Difficulty, Goal Specificity and Duration of Practice Time Intervals
on Muscular Endurance Performance." *Journal of Sports Sciences* 15
(2): 125–35.

Latham, Gary P., and Edwin A. Locke. 1991. "Self-Regulation through
Goal Setting." *Organizational Behavior and Human Decision Processes* 50
(2): 212–47.

Healy, Laura, Alison Tincknell-Smith, and Nikos Ntoumanis. 2018. "Goal
Setting in Sport and Performance." *Oxford Research Encyclopedia of
Psychology.* https://doi.org/10.1093/acrefore/9780190236557.013.152.

Lunenburg, Fred C. 2011. "Goal-Setting Theory of Motivation."
International Journal of Management, Business, and Administration
15 (1): 1–6.

Radosevich, David J., Mark R. Allyn, and Seokhwa Yun. 2007. "Goal
Orientation and Goal Setting: Predicting Performance by Integrating

Four-Factor Goal Orientation Theory with Goal Setting Processes." *Seoul Journal of Business.* https://doi.org/10.35152/snusjb.2007.13.1.002.

Ward, Phillip. 2011. "Goal Setting and Performance Feedback." *Behavioral Sport Psychology.* https://doi.org/10.1007/978-1-4614-0070-7_6.

The Science of Habit Formation

Burchard, Brendon. 2017. *High Performance Habits: How Extraordinary People Become That Way.* Hay House, Inc.

Clear, James. 2018. *Atomic Habits: An Easy & Proven Way to Build Good Habits & Break Bad Ones.* Penguin.

Fogg, B. J. 2019. *Tiny Habits: The Small Changes That Change Everything.* Houghton Mifflin Harcourt.

Lieber, Megan. 2016. "Implementing Tiny Goals after Current Habits to Create Consistent Healthy Lifestyle Routine." The University of Akron. https://ideaexchange.uakron.edu/honors_research_projects/343/.

Lally, Phillippa, Cornelia H. M. van Jaarsveld, Henry W. W. Potts, and Jane Wardle. 2010. "How Are Habits Formed: Modelling Habit Formation in the Real World." *European Journal of Social Psychology* 40 (6): 998–1009.

Chapter 5: What is Flow

Benson, Herbert, and William Proctor. 2004. *The Breakout Principle: How to Activate the Natural Trigger That Maximizes Creativity, Athletic Performance, Productivity, and Personal Well-Being.* Simon and Schuster. Pg. 4-25

Czikszentmihalyi, Mihaly. 1990. "Flow: The Psychology of Optimal Experience." New York: Harper & Row. http://vedpuriswar.org/bookReviews/Leadership/Flow.pdf.

De Kock, Frederick Gideon. 2014. "The Neuropsychological Measure (EEG) of Flow under Conditions of Peak Performance." University of South Africa. https://pdfs.semanticscholar.org/88ee/ea1f774dd83ac1855f55c9311052b729c273.pdf.

Dietrich, Arne. 2003. "Functional Neuroanatomy of Altered States of Consciousness: The Transient Hypofrontality Hypothesis." *Consciousness and Cognition* 12 (2): 231–56.

"Neurocognitive Mechanisms Underlying the Experience of Flow." *Consciousness and Cognition* 13 (4): 746–61. 2004

Kawabata, Masato, and Clifford J. Mallett. 2011. "Flow Experience in Physical Activity: Examination of the Internal Structure of Flow from a Process-Related Perspective." *Motivation and Emotion* 35 (4): 393–402.

Kotler, Steven, and Jamie Wheal. 2017. *Stealing Fire: How Silicon Valley, the Navy SEALs, and Maverick Scientists Are Revolutionizing the Way We Live and Work.* HarperCollins.

Nakamura, Jeanne, and Mihaly Csikszentmihalyi. 2009. "Flow Theory and Research." *Handbook of Positive Psychology,* 195–206.

"The Concept of Flow." In *Flow and the Foundations of Positive Psychology: The Collected Works of Mihaly Csikszentmihalyi,* edited by Mihaly Csikszentmihalyi, 239–63. Dordrecht: Springer Netherlands. 2014

Nideffer, Robert M. 2002. "Getting Into The Optimal Performance State." *Enhanced Performance Systems,* 184–204.

https://www.washingtonpost.com/lifestyle/wellness/ its-great-to-be-in-the-zone—while-working-exercising-and-creating-ar t-heres-how-to-get-there; Jessica Wapner, April 9, 2019

Chapter 6: Setting the Table for Flow

Baumann, Nicola. 2012. "Autotelic Personality." In *Advances in Flow Research,* edited by Stefan Engeser, 165–86. New York, NY: Springer New York.

Czikszentmihalyi, Mihaly. 1990. "Flow: The Psychology of Optimal Experience." New York: Harper & Row. http://vedpuriswar.org/ bookReviews/Leadership/Flow.pdf. Pgs. 72-116

Baumann, Nicola, and David Scheffer. 2011. "Seeking Flow in the Achievement Domain: The Achievement Flow Motive behind Flow Experience." *Motivation and Emotion* 35 (3): 267–84.

Jackson, Susan A. 1995. "Factors Influencing the Occurrence of Flow State in Elite Athletes." *Journal of Applied Sport Psychology* 7 (2): 138–66.

Kowal, John, and Michelle S. Fortier. 1999. "Motivational Determinants of Flow: Contributions From Self-Determination Theory." *The Journal of Social Psychology* 139 (3): 355–68.

Harris, David J., Samuel J. Vine, and Mark R. Wilson. 2017. "Neurocognitive Mechanisms of the Flow State." *Progress in Brain Research* 234 (July): 221–43.

Koehn, Stefan. 2007. "Propensity and Attainment of Flow State." Phd, Victoria University. http://vuir.vu.edu.au/1535/.

Benson, Herbert, and William Proctor. 2004. *The Breakout Principle: How to Activate the Natural Trigger That Maximizes Creativity, Athletic Performance, Productivity, and Personal Well-Being.* Simon and Schuster, pp 26-45

Kotler, Steven, and Jamie Wheal. 2017. *Stealing Fire: How Silicon Valley, the Navy SEALs, and Maverick Scientists Are Revolutionizing the Way We Live and Work*. HarperCollins. Pp 212-215

Csikszentmihalyi, Mihaly. 2018. "Getting in the Zone, Part 1: Flow and Finding a State of Peak Performance." *Journal of Singing: The Official Journal of the National Association of Teachers of Singing* 74 (3): 329–34.

Fullagar, Clive J., Patrick A. Knight, and Heather S. Sovern. 2013. "Challenge/skill Balance, Flow, and Performance Anxiety." *Applied Psychology = Psychologie Appliquee* 62 (2): 236–59.

Lambert, Joseph, and Mihaly Csikszentmihalyi. 2020. "Facilitating or Foiling Flow: The Role of Momentary Perceptions of Feedback." *The Journal of Positive Psychology* 15 (2): 208–19.

Nideffer, Robert M. 2002. "Getting Into The Optimal Performance State." *Enhanced Performance Systems*, 184–204.

"Stefan_Engeser__Anja_Schiepe-Tiska_auth.__Stefan_Engeser_eds._ Advances_in_Flow_Research__1_.pdf." n.d.pp 51-62

Chapter 7: Flow Has a Cycle - Respect It For More Flow

Keller, Johannes, and Anne Landhäußer. 2012. "The Flow Model Revisited." In *Advances in Flow Research*, edited by Stefan Engeser, 51–64. New York, NY: Springer New York.

Bricteux, Céline, Jose Navarro, Lucía Ceja, and Guillaume Fuerst. 2017. "Interest as a Moderator in the Relationship Between Challenge/Skills Balance and Flow at Work: An Analysis at Within-Individual Level." *Journal of Happiness Studies* 18 (3): 861–80.

Benson, Herbert, and William Proctor. 2004. *The Breakout Principle: How to Activate the Natural Trigger That Maximizes Creativity, Athletic Performance, Productivity, and Personal Well-Being*. Simon and Schuster pg 48-63.

Chapter 8: Free Your Brain for Flow

Your Brain is a Horrible File Cabinet—Reducing Cognitive Load

Barrouillet, Pierre, Sophie Bernardin, Sophie Portrat, Evie Vergauwe, and Valérie Camos. 2007. "Time and Cognitive Load in Working Memory." *Journal of Experimental Psychology. Learning, Memory, and Cognition* 33 (3): 570–85.

Camos, Valérie, and Sophie Portrat. 2015. "The Impact of Cognitive Load on Delayed Recall." *Psychonomic Bulletin & Review* 22 (4): 1029–34.

Chen, I., Chi-Cheng Chang, and Others. 2009. "Cognitive Load Theory: An Empirical Study of Anxiety and Task Performance in Language Learning." http://repositorio.ual.es/bitstream/handle/10835/759/Art_18_348.pdf?sequence=1.

Gilchrist, Amanda L. 2015. "How Should We Measure Chunks? A Continuing Issue in Chunking Research and a Way Forward." *Frontiers in Psychology* 6 (September): 1456.

Miller, G. A. 1956. "The Magical Number Seven plus or Minus Two: Some Limits on Our Capacity for Processing Information." *Psychological Review* 63 (2): 81–97.

Change Your Time Perception

Bryan, Judith F., and Edwin A. Locke. 1967. "Parkinson's Law as a Goal-Setting Phenomenon." *Organizational Behavior and Human Performance* 2 (3): 258–75.

Wikipedia contributors. (2020, April 27). Parkinson's law. In Wikipedia, The Free Encyclopedia. Retrieved 22:25, May 5, 2020, from https://en.wikipedia.org/w/index.php?title=Parkinson%27s_law&oldid=953403322

A Tiny Way to Change Your Behavior

Fogg, B. J. 2019. *Tiny Habits: The Small Changes That Change Everything.* Houghton Mifflin Harcourt.

Volini, Erica, Schwartz, Jeff, Denny, Brad, *"Designing work for well-being." May 15, 2020.* Deloitte Insights

Chapter 9: Avoid Burnout: Become A Corporate Athlete

Loehr, J., and T. Schwartz. 2001. "The Making of a Corporate Athlete." *Harvard Business Review* 79 (1): 120–28, 176.

Lee, R. T., and B. E. Ashforth. 1990. "On the Meaning of Maslach's Three Dimensions of Burnout." *The Journal of Applied Psychology* 75 (6): 743–47.

Leiter, M. P., C. Maslach, and K. Frame. 2014. "Burnout." In *The Encyclopedia of Clinical Psychology,* edited by Robin L. Cautin and Scott O. Lilienfeld, 87:1–7. Hoboken, NJ, USA: John Wiley & Sons, Inc.

Moen, Phyllis, Erin L. Kelly, and Jack Lam. 2013. "Healthy Work Revisited: Do Changes in Time Strain Predict Well-Being?" *Journal of Occupational Health Psychology* 18 (2): 157–72.

Moen, Phyllis, Jack Lam, Samantha Ammons, and Erin L. Kelly. 2013. "Time Work by Overworked Professionals: Strategies in Response to the Stress of Higher Status." *Work and Occupations* 40 (2): 79–114.

Perlow, Leslie A., and Jessica L. Porter. 2009. "Making Time off Predictable—and Required." *Harvard Business Review* 87 (10): 102–9, 142.

Virtanen, M., J. E. Ferrie, A. Singh-Manoux, M. J. Shipley, S. A. Stansfeld, M. G. Marmot, K. Ahola, J. Vahtera, and M. Kivimäki. 2011. "Long Working Hours and Symptoms of Anxiety and Depression: A 5-Year Follow-up of the Whitehall II Study." *Psychological Medicine* 41 (12): 2485–94.

Chapter 10: Your Addiction to Distraction is Costing You Your Dream

Gazzaley, Adam, and Larry D. Rosen. 2016a. "The Distracted Mind." *Ancient Brains in a High-Tech World.* http://www.cs.uni.edu/~jacobson/1025/17/The-Distracted-Mind.pdf.

Goodman, Aviel. 2008. "Neurobiology of Addiction. An Integrative Review." *Biochemical Pharmacology* 75 (1): 266–322.

Hallowell, Edward M. 2005. "Overloaded Circuits." *Harvard Business Review*, 11.

Killingsworth, Matthew A., and Daniel T. Gilbert. 2010. "A Wandering Mind Is an Unhappy Mind." *Science* 330 (6006): 932.

Newport, C. 2016. "[Deep Work]." Hachette UK. 2016. https://www.researchgate.net/profile/Lalatendu_Jena/publication/322593033_Book_Review_Deep_Work_Rules_for_Focused_Success_in_a_Distracted_World_by_Cal_Newport_Piatkus-

Newport, Cal. 2019. *Digital Minimalism: Choosing a Focused Life in a Noisy World.* Penguin.

Stephenson, Mitchell. 2019. "Deep Work: Dealing With Distractions in a Distracting World." https://www.soa.org/globalassets/assets/library/newsletters/actuary-of-the-future/2019/may/aof-2019-iss44-stephenson.pdf.

Chapter 11: Engineering Flow into Your Daily Routine

https://en.wikipedia.org/wiki/Michel_Lotito

Ibid

https://commonplacefacts.wordpress.com/2019/06/19/
meet-the-man-who-ate-an-entire-airplane/

A Goal Setting System for Elite Performance

Latham, Gary P., and Edwin A. Locke. 1991. "Self-Regulation through
Goal Setting." *Organizational Behavior and Human Decision Processes* 50
(2): 212–47.

Bar-Eli, M., G. Tenenbaum, J. S. Pie, Y. Btesh, and A. Almog. 1997. "Effect
of Goal Difficulty, Goal Specificity and Duration of Practice Time Intervals
on Muscular Endurance Performance." *Journal of Sports Sciences* 15
(2): 125–35.

Lunenburg, Fred C. 2011. "Goal-Setting Theory of Motivation."
International Journal of Management, Business, and Administration
15 (1): 1–6.

Elite Performance Demands Execution

Bossidy, Larry, Ram Charan, and Charles Burck. 2004. "Execution: The
Discipline of Getting Things Done." *Afp Exchange* 24 (1): 26–29.

Taylor, Alex, III. 2009. "Fixing up FORD." *CNN Money [online].*
Retrieved from Http://money. Cnn. com/2009/05/11/news/companies/
mulally_ford. Fortune/index. Htm. https://brainmass.com/file/280277/
Fixing+up+Ford.docx.

Welbourne, T. 2005. "Leaders Talk about Executing Strategy." *Leadership*
Pulse. https://www.leadershippulse.com/wp-content/uploads/2018/10/
ExecutingStrategy.pdf.

Constructing Your Day for Flow

Breus, Michael. 2016. *The Power of When: Discover Your Chronotype—and*
the Best Time to Eat Lunch, Ask for a Raise, Have Sex, Write a Novel, Take
Your Meds, and More. Little, Brown.

Matchock, Robert L., and J. Toby Mordkoff. 2009. "Chronotype and
Time-of-Day Influences on the Alerting, Orienting, and Executive

Components of Attention." *Experimental Brain Research. Experimentelle Hirnforschung. Experimentation Cerebrale* 192 (2): 189–98.

Schmidt, Christina, Fabienne Collette, Christian Cajochen, and Philippe Peigneux. 2007. "A Time to Think: Circadian Rhythms in Human Cognition." *Cognitive Neuropsychology* 24 (7): 755–89.

Vitale, Jacopo Antonino, and Andi Weydahl. 2017. "Chronotype, Physical Activity, and Sport Performance: A Systematic Review." *Sports Medicine* 47 (9): 1859–68.

Chapter 12: *Leveraging Individual Performance Through Group Flow*

Elite Performance in Business Through Flow (Use Kallman models with Pink and move strengths based thinking and citations to this chapter. From chapter 11

Finding Success by Putting Company Culture First: April 19, 2011, Diane Ransom, https://www.entrepreneur.com/article/219509

Kallman, T., & Kallman, A. (2018). Flow: Get Everyone Moving in the Right Direction...And Loving It. Morgan James Publishing, pp. 12-38

Pink, D. H. (2011). *Drive: The Surprising Truth About What Motivates Us*. Penguin.

Bakker, Arnold B., and Marianne van Woerkom. 2017. "Flow at Work: A Self-Determination Perspective." *Occupational Health Science* 1 (1): 47–65.

Demerouti, Evangelia, and Anne Mäkikangas. 2017. "What Predicts Flow at Work?: Theoretical and Empirical Perspectives." In *Flow at Work*, 66–80. Routledge.

Fullagar, Clive J., and E. Kevin Kelloway. 2009. "Flow at Work: An Experience Sampling Approach." *Journal of Occupational and Organizational Psychology* 82 (3): 595–615.

Hout, Jef J. J. van den, Orin C. Davis, and Bob Walrave. 2016. "The Application of Team Flow Theory." In *Flow Experience: Empirical Research and Applications*, edited by László Harmat, Frans Ørsted Andersen, Fredrik Ullén, Jon Wright, and Gaynor Sadlo, 233–47. Cham: Springer International Publishing.

Sawyer, Keith. 2015. "Group Flow and Group Genius." *NAMTA Journal* 40 (3): 29–52.

Simmons, Mathias J. 2015. "The Relationship between Leadership and Flow: A Daily Diary Study." Kansas State University. http://krex.k-state.edu/dspace/handle/2097/18822.

"Stefan_Engeser__Anja_Schiepe-Tiska_auth.__Stefan_Engeser_eds._Advances_in_Flow_Research__1_.pdf." n.d.pp 99-100

Preparing Your Children For the 21ˢᵗ Century Through Flow

Czikszentmihalyi, Mihaly. 1990. "Flow: The Psychology of Optimal Experience." New York: Harper & Row. http://vedpuriswar.org/bookReviews/Leadership/Flow.pdf.

Larsen, Jacob R. Kirkegaard. 2013. "Family Flow: The Pleasures of 'Being Together' in a Holiday Home." *Scandinavian Journal of Hospitality and Tourism* 13 (3): 153–74.

Chapter 13: Return on Your Flow Investment

https://www2.deloitte.com/us/en/insights/topics/talent/future-workforce-engagement-in-the-workplace.html

https://www.psychologytoday.com/us/blog/the-playing-field/201402/flow-states-and-creativity

https://www.cwilsonmeloncelli.com/490-improvement-learning-speed-darpa/

https://hbr.org/2014/05/create-a-work-environment-that-fosters-flow

https://www.forbes.com/sites/bruceupbin/2011/12/13/five-new-management-metrics-you-need-to-know/#44eceeaa717d
(#1 metric: % time spent in flow state)

Chapter 14 The Answer to Exponential Change is Flow— Not Squeezing Harder

http://csef.ru/en/politica-i-geopolitica/510/chto-nas-zhdyot-v-xxi-veke-futurologicheskij-prognoz-reya-kurczvejla-8874

"Law of Accelerating Returns"; Ray Kurzweil, "The Law of Accelerating Returns," March 7, 2001. See: https://singularityhub.com/2016/03/22/technology-feels-like-its-accelerating-because-it-actually-is/

Brynjolfsson, Erik, and Andrew McAfee. 2011. *Race Against the Machine: How the Digital Revolution Is Accelerating Innovation, Driving Productivity, and Irreversibly Transforming Employment and the Economy*. Brynjolfsson and McAfee.

Diamandis, Peter H., and Steven Kotler. 2020. The Future Is Faster Than You Think: How Converging Technologies Are Transforming Business, Industries, and Our Lives. Simon and Schuster. Pp 8-12.

https://www.mckinsey.com/featured-insights/future-of-work/skill-shift-automation-and-the-future-of-the-workforce

https://hbr.org/2018/01/how-automation-will-change-work-purpose-and-meaning